Keto Bread

And

Keto Chaffle Cookbook

2 Books in 1

The Best Step By Step Guide To Make A Low-Carb, Gluten Free Keto Bread and Chaffle For Lose Weight and Improve Health

By

Emily Baker

TABLE OF CONTENTS

ESSENTIAL KETO BREAD

KETO CHAFFLE COOKBOOK

Essential Keto Bread

The Best Keto Cookbook With Tasty recipes For Cooking a Low-Carb And Gluten Free Bread For Lose Weight

By

Emily Baker

Introduction

Ketogenic refers to a low-carbohydrate diet. The aim is to eat more calories from fat and protein while eating fewer calories from carbohydrates. The carbohydrates that are easiest to digest, such as starch, pastries, soda, and white bread, are the first to go. When you consume fewer than 50 g of carbohydrates a day, your body easily runs out of energy. This normally takes three or four days. Then you'll begin to break down fat and protein for energy, potentially resulting in weight loss. Ketosis is the term for this state. It's crucial to remember that the ketogenic diet is a short-term diet designed to help you lose weight rather than change your lifestyle. A ketogenic diet is more often used to reduce weight, although it may also be used to treat medical problems such as epilepsy. It can even benefit those suffering from heart failure, some brain disorders, and even acne, although further study is required. Since the keto diet contains too much fat, adherents must ingest fat at every meal time. In a normal 2K-calorie diet, that would seem like 165 g of fat, 40 g of carbohydrates, and 75 g of protein. The exact ratio, on the other hand, is determined by your basic requirements. Nuts (walnuts, almonds), avocados, seeds, olive oil and tofu are among the healthier unsaturated fats allowed on the keto diet. However, oils (coconut, palm), butter, lard, and peanut butter all contain high amounts of saturated fats. Protein is an essential aspect of the keto diet, although it is also difficult to discern between protein items that are lean and protein products rich in fat(saturated), such as beef, bacon, and pork. What for fruits and vegetables? While fruits are generally rich in carbohydrates, unique fruits may be obtained in limited quantities (generally berries) Leafy greens (like kale, chard, Swiss chard, and spinach), broccoli, cauliflower, asparagus, tomatoes, brussels sprouts, bell peppers, garlic, cucumbers, mushrooms, summer squashes, as well as celery are also rich in carbohydrates. One cup of sliced broccoli includes about six carbohydrates. At the same time, there are several possible keto hazards, such as liver deficiency, liver complications, constipation, kidney disorders, and so on. As a result, we can also keep our Keto diet portions in check.

Understanding The Ketogenic Diet

This chapter delves into the Ketogenic diet in depth. The chapter further discusses which foods to consume on the Keto diet and which foods to stop while on this diet. The Keto diet is often explained in-depth, including how it functions and what health advantages it provides.

The ketogenic diet (or keto diet) is a high-fat, low-carbohydrate diet with various health benefits. Evidently, more than 20 studies suggest that this form of diet will help you lose weight and boost your wellbeing. Diabetes patients, epilepsy patients, patients suffering from Alzheimer's disease, as well as cancer can all benefit from ketogenic diets.

1.1 What is Keto?

The ketogenic diet is a very low carbohydrate, high-fat diet that has a lot in common with the Atkins diet and other low-carb diets. It necessitates a significant reduction of carbohydrate consumption and a replacement with fat. This reduction of carbohydrates puts the body into a metabolic condition known as ketosis. As this occurs, the body's energy production of fat-burning skyrockets. In addition, it converts fat into ketones in the liver, which will supply energy to the brain. Ketogenic diets can result in substantial reductions in insulin as well as blood sugar levels. This, along with the increased ketones, has numerous health benefits.

Ketogenic Diets Come in Many Forms
There are a few variations of the ketogenic diet, including:
The traditional ketogenic diet consists of a diet that is low in carbs, mild in protein, and strong in fats. It usually has a 75 percent fat content, a 5% carbohydrate content, and a 20% protein content.
The cyclic ketogenic diet entails high-carb reefed cycles, such as five ketogenic days accompanied by two days of high carbohydrate use.

A ketogenic diet with particular goals: The diet requires carbs to be inserted in between exercises.

Protein-rich ketogenic diet: This is comparable to a normal keto diet, but it contains extra protein. Usually, the ratio is 60 percent fat, 5% sugars, and 35 percent protein. However, only normal and protein-rich ketogenic diets have been extensively studied. More complex keto diets, such as targeted or cyclic keto, are mainly utilized by bodybuilders and athletes.

Ketogenic Diet Health Benefits

In fact, the keto diet first gained popularity as a means of treating neurological conditions, such as epilepsy. Following that, research has shown that diet can help with a broad variety of health issues:

Heart disease: The keto diet has been found to decrease risk factors such as body fat, blood sugar, HDL cholesterol and blood pressure.

Alzheimer's disease: The ketogenic diet can ease Alzheimer's symptoms while still delaying the disease's progression.

Epilepsy: Research has demonstrated that a ketogenic diet can significantly reduce seizures in children with epileptic seizures.

Cancer: The diet is actually being used to control a number of diseases and to delay tumor development.

Acne: Lower insulin levels, as well as less sugar or fried food diets, will aid acne recovery.

Parkinson's disease: According to one report, diet can help relieve the effects of Parkinson's disease.

Brain injuries: One study found that the diet would also increase concussions and improve recovery after a brain injury.

Polycystic ovary syndrome: A ketogenic diet may help lower insulin levels and can be helpful in the treatment of polycystic ovary syndrome.

What foods can you consume on a ketogenic diet?

The majority of your meals will revolve around the following foods:

- Salmon, mackerel and tuna are representations of fatty fish.
- Look for pastured eggs, whole eggs, or omega-3 eggs.
- Seek for grass-fed butter plus cream wherever possible.
- Red meat, ham, sausage, turkey, bacon, chicken and steak are all examples of meat.
- Non-processed cheese (goat, cheddar, mozzarella, blue, or cream).
- Flax seeds, walnuts, almonds, pumpkin seeds, chia seeds and other nuts and beans
- Avocado oil, olive oil and coconut oil are the other safe oils.
- Salt, spices and pepper, as well as a variety of herbs, may be used as condiments.
- Avocados: entire avocados or guacamole made freshly.
- Low-carb vegetables including greens, tomatoes, onions, peppers and other related veggies.

Foods to avoid on a ketogenic diet include:

Carbohydrate-rich diets can be avoided as much as possible.

The following is a selection of items that must be eliminated or reduced on a ketogenic diet:

- Sugary drink, ice cream, soda, smoothies, cake, candy and other sugary items
- Wheat, pasta, cereals, rice, and other wheat-based products are examples of starches or grains.
- Sweet potatoes, parsnips, parsnips, potatoes, carrots and other tubers & root vegetables
- Reduced-calorie or low-fat foods are extremely processed and abundant in carbohydrates.
- Fruit: All fruits, with the exception of tiny bits of berries like strawberries.
- Chickpeas, lentils, peas, kidney beans, and other legumes or beans
- Some sauces/condiments: They are also high in unhealthy fat and sugar.

- Unhealthy fats: Limit the intake to mayonnaise, processed vegetable oils, and other processed fats.
- Alcohol: Because of their carb content, certain alcoholic beverages will shake you out of ketosis.
- Dietary ingredients that are sugar-free: Alcohols, which are often rich in sugar, may influence ketone levels in certain situations. These objects seem to have passed through a lot of refining as well.

1.2 What is the Keto diet, and how does it work?

The "ketogenic" keto diet consists of consuming a moderate level of protein, a heavy amount of fat, and relatively little carbohydrates; also, the fruit is forbidden. As for every diet fad, the advantages to adherents include improved vitality, weight reduction, and mental clarity. Is the ketogenic diet, though, what it's cracked up to be?

Dietitians and nutritionists are quiet on the topic. Low-carb diets like keto appear to assist with weight loss in the short term, but they are no more successful than any other self-help or conventional diet. They still don't seem to be enhancing athletic results.

The ketogenic diet was created to treat epilepsy instead of losing weight. In the 1920s, physicians found that holding people on low-carb diets induced their bodies to use fat as the predominant fuel source rather than glucose. When only fat is available for the body to combust or burn, the body converts fats to fatty acids, which are then converted to ketones, which can be used and taken up to power the body's cells.

Currently, feeding the body exclusively ketones prevents epilepsy for unclear causes. However, with the advent of anti-seizure medicines, few patients with epilepsy rely on ketogenic diets anymore, while certain people who may not respond to medications may benefit. Low carb diets like the Atkins diet, which gained popularity in the early 2000s, also spawned keto diets for weight loss. In comparison, all groups of meatier-meal diets restrict carbohydrates. This diet does not have a set structure, although most routines provide for fewer than fifty grams of carbs per day.

A keto diet causes the body to enter a state known as ketosis, in which the body's cells become completely reliant on ketones for nutrition. It's not exactly clear that this leads to weight loss, but ketosis decreases appetite and can affect hunger-controlling hormones, including insulin. As a consequence, proteins and fats can keep humans fuller longer than sugars, resulting in lower net calorie intake.

In one head-to-head comparison, researchers looked at 48 separate diet trials in which subjects were randomly allocated to one of the well-known diets. Low-carb diets like South Beach, Atkins, and Zone, as well as low-fat diets like Ornish diets and portion restriction diets like Weight Watchers and Jenny Craig, were among the options.

Every diet resulted in greater weight loss than almost no diet after six months, according to the results. Low-carb and low-fat dieters lost almost equal amounts of weight as compared to non-dieters, with low-carb dieters losing 19 pounds on average versus low-fat dieters dropping 17.6 pounds (7.99 kilograms). At 12 months, both diet styles displayed symptoms of dropping off, with low-fat and low-carb dieters being 16 pounds (7.27 kg) smaller on average than non-dieters.

There were few differences in weight reduction within the diets of designated people. This is in line with the practice of recommending every diet that an individual practice in order to lose weight.

Another study of well-known diets discovered the Atkins diet, which results in greater weight loss than merely teaching people about portion control. Nevertheless, several of the scientific researched about this low-carb diet featured licensed dietitians assisting respondents in making food decisions, rather than the self-directed approach used by most people. This has been seen in other diet studies, according to the researchers, and the tests' results seem to be more positive in the real world than the weight loss.

Finally, a simple comparison between low-carb versus low-fat dieting revealed that there was a statistically significant difference in the amount of weight lost over a year. Low-carbohydrate dieters dropped an average of 13 pounds (6 kg), compared to 11.7 pounds for low-fat dieters (5.3 kg).

Ketogenic diets may help us lose weight, but they are no more successful than other diet methods. Since carbohydrate reserves in the body comprise water molecules, the bulk of the weight lost during the early stages of a ketogenic diet is water weight. This gives the scale an exciting amount at first, but weight reduction slows down with time.

What are the keto effects, and how can they help?

The advantages of a keto diet are close to that of other high-fat, low-carb diets, but it tends to be more successful than centrist low-carb diets. Keto is a low-carb, high-fat diet that maximizes health benefits. However, it will slightly raise the likelihood of complications.

Aid in weight loss

Weight reduction can be improved by converting the body into a fat-burning device. Insulin levels – the hormone that retains fat – are falling rapidly, suggesting that fat burning has risen dramatically. This seems to make it much easier to lose bodyweight without going hungry.

More than thirty high-quality observational studies show that low-carb and keto diets are more effective than other diets at losing weight.

Reverse type 2 diabetes by regulating blood sugar

A ketogenic diet has been shown in research to be successful in the treatment of type 2 diabetes, with total disease reversal occurring in certain instances. It makes perfect sense since keto removes the need for therapy, lowers blood sugar levels, and eliminates the potential negative consequences of high insulin levels.

Since a keto diet will reverse type 2 diabetes, it is likely to be helpful in preventing and reversing pre-diabetes. Keep in mind that "reversal" in this context refers to changing the disease, improving glucose tolerance, and reducing the need for care. It may be so drastically altered that after therapy, blood pressure returns to normal with time. In this context, reversal refers to progressing or deteriorating in the reverse direction of the condition. Changes in your lifestyle, on the other side, just succeed if you bring them into effect. If a person returns to the way of life he or she has before diabetes type 2 appeared and advanced, it is possible that success would return with time.

Improve your mental and physical performance:
Some people use ketogenic diets to boost their mental performance. It's also normal for people to feel more energized while they're in ketosis.
They don't need nutritional carbs for the brain on keto. It runs on ketones 24 hours a day, seven days a week, with a small amount of glucose synthesized in the liver. Carbohydrates are not necessary for the diet. As a result, ketosis leads to a steady flow of food (ketones) to the brain, avoiding significant blood sugar spikes. This will also assist with improved focus and attention, as well as clearing brain fog and improving mental awareness.

Epilepsy Treatment

The keto diet has been used to manage epilepsy since the 19th and 20th centuries and has proved to be effective. It has historically been used mainly for adolescents, although in recent years, it has also proved to be useful to adults. Or, used in conjunction with a keto diet, certain people with epilepsy might be able to take less to no anti-epileptic drugs while being seizure-free. This may help to reduce the drug's adverse effects while still improving cognitive capacity.

Keto Bread Recipes

1 Empanadas

(Ready in about 35 minutes | Serving 4 | Difficulty: Moderate)

Per serving: Kcal 554, Fat: 48g, Net Carbs: 7g, Protein: 19g

Ingredients

- 11/4 cups of almond flour
- 1/2 tsp of cream of tartar
- 1 tsp of whipping cream
- 1 tsp of baking powder
- 1 tsp of xanthan gum
- 2 tbsp of butter
- 2 eggs
- 2 tbsp of ricotta cheese

Instructions

Mix everything except half of the eggs in a bowl. Knead using the mixer's hook attachment until a ball of dough is formed. Use plastic film to wrap it and place it in the fridge for around an hour. Make squared of parchment paper. Take the dough out and dice it into pieces and make a ball out of each piece. Press every ball between 2 pieces of paper to form a flat disk. Peel the paper on the top side and use it for the rest of the balls. Split the rest of the egg into white and yolk. Whisk heavy cream and yolk. Brush balls with it and place them on a baking tray. Bake for around 20 minutes at 300 degrees F.

2 Keto bagels

(Ready in about 25 minutes | Serving 4 | Difficulty: Easy)

Per serving: Kcal 477, Fat: 39g, Net Carbs: 4g, Protein: 23g

Ingredients

Bagels

- 1 egg
- 7 oz. of mozzarella cheese
- 11/2 cups of almond flour
- 1 oz. of cream cheese
- 2 tsp of baking powder

Topping

- 1 tsp of sesame seeds
- 2 tsp of flaxseed
- 1/2 tsp of sea salt
- 1 egg
- 1/4 tsp of poppy seeds

Instructions

Preheat oven to around 430 degrees F. Line parchment paper in the baking tray. Microwave cream cheese and mozzarella in a bowl for around 1 minute. Whisk baking powder and flour in another bowl. Add egg with this mixture into cheese. Whisk to form a dough. Divide dough into 4 parts and make bun shapes. Place on a tray and form a hole in the center using the thumb. Place seasoning and seeds in a bowl and stir. Beat one more egg in a bowl and brush bagel with it. Sprinkle seasoning and bake for around 15 minutes.

© MidgetMomma.com

3 Hot dog buns

(Ready in about 1 hour | Serving 10 | Difficulty: Hard)

Per serving: Kcal 311, Fat: 8g, Net Carbs: 1g, Protein: 4g

Ingredients

- 11/4 cups of almond flour
- 2 tsp of baking powder
- 1/3 cup of psyllium husk ground
- 1 tsp of sea salt
- 11/4 cups of boiling water
- 2 tsp of cider vinegar
- 3 eggs, only whites

Instructions

Preheat oven to around 350 degrees F. Mix dry ingredients using a bowl. Boil water and add egg whites and vinegar in a bowl and mix for around 30 seconds using a hand mixer. Make 10 pieces out of dough and roll into the shape of hot dog buns. Place in a tray and bake for around 50 minutes.

4 Cornbread

(Ready in about 25 minutes | Serving 8 | Difficulty: Easy)

Per serving: Kcal 237, Fat: 23g, Net Carbs: 1g, Protein: 7g

Ingredients

- 1/4 cup of coconut flour
- 1/3 cup of whey protein
- 1/3 cup of oat fiber
- 11/2 tsp of baking powder
- 4 oz. melted butter
- 1/4 tsp of salt
- 1/3 cup of bacon fat
- 4 eggs
- 1/4 cup of water
- 1/4 tsp corn of extract

Instructions

Preheat oven to around 350 degrees F. Oil a pan and warm in the oven. Mix dry ingredients using a bowl and add the rest of the ingredients except corn extract. Beat using a hand mixer and add corn extract. Pour mixture into the pan and bake for around 20 minutes.

5 Quick style bread

(Ready in about 15 minutes | Serving 4 | Difficulty: Easy)

Per serving: Kcal 303, Fat: 26g, Net Carbs: 5g, Protein: 10g

Ingredients

- 2 pinches of salt
- 2 oz. of cream cheese
- 2 tsp of psyllium husk ground
- 2 eggs, only whites
- 1/2 cup of almond flour
- 1/4 cup of sunflower seeds
- 1/2 cup of sesame seeds
- 11/2 tsp of baking powder

Instructions

Preheat oven to around 400 degrees F. Mix cream cheese and egg whites in a bowl. Add the rest of the ingredients and mix. Shape squares of the mixture and bake for around 12 minutes by placing them in the pan.

6 Mediterranean bread

(Ready in about 30 minutes | Serving 6 | Difficulty: Easy)

Per serving: Kcal 139, Fat: 12g, Net Carbs: 1g, Protein: 4g

Ingredients

- 1/2 cup of coconut flour
- 1/4 cup of olive oil
- 1/2 tbsp of black peppercorns
- 1 tbsp of psyllium husk ground
- 1 cup of boiling water
- 1/2 tsp of sea salt
- 1/2 cup of shredded parmesan
- 1/4 tsp of granulated garlic
- 1/2 tbsp of dried rosemary

Instructions

Mix dry ingredients in a bowl and add cheese and oil. Add warm water at last and stir. Line baking sheet with parchment paper and flatten dough on it. Roll out the dough to make it thin. Bake for around 25 minutes at 350 degrees F.

7 Parmesan croutons

(Ready in about 1 hour | Serving 8 | Difficulty: Hard)

Per serving: Kcal 259, Fat: 23g, Net Carbs: 1g, Protein: 8g

Ingredients

- 4 oz. of butter
- 11/4 cups of almond flour
- 3/4 cup of shredded Parmesan
- 1/3 cup of psyllium husk powder
- 1 tsp of sea salt
- 2 tsp of baking powder
- 2 tsp of cider vinegar
- 3 eggs, only whites
- 11/4 cups of boiling water

Instructions

Preheat oven to around 350 degrees F. Add dry ingredients to a bowl and mix. Boil water and add to dry ingredients with egg whites and vinegar. Beat for around 30 seconds. Form flat pieces (8) out of dough and bake for around 40 minutes in the lower rack. Split pieces of bread lengthwise and place on sheet pan face up. Stir parmesan cheese and butter and spread on bread. Broil for around 5 minutes at 450 degrees F.

8 Cloud bread

(Ready in about 30 minutes | Serving 2 | Difficulty: Easy)

Per serving: Kcal 740, Fat: 61g, Net Carbs: 7g, Protein: 37g

Ingredients

- 3 eggs
- 1 pinch of salt
- 4 oz. of cream cheese
- 1/2 tbsp of psyllium husk ground
- 1/4 tsp of cream of tartar
- 1/2 tsp of baking powder

Instructions

Preheat oven to around 300 degrees F. Add egg yolks to one bowl and whites to another. Mix salt in whites and add the rest of the ingredients to yolks. Mix two bowls and place them on a baking tray lined with paper. Spread into circles and bake for around 25 minutes.

9 Garlic focaccia

(Ready in about 25 minutes | Serving 8 | Difficulty: Easy)

Per serving: Kcal 196, Fat: 17g, Net Carbs: 2g, Protein: 8g

Ingredients

Foccacia

- 2 tbsp of cream cheese
- 11/2 cups of shredded cheese mozzarella
- 1 tsp of white wine vinegar
- 1/2 tsp of garlic powder
- 3/4 cup of almond flour
- 1 egg
- 1/2 tsp of salt

Butter

- 1/2 tsp chopped fresh rosemary
- 3 chopped garlic cloves
- 2 oz. of butter
- 1/2 tsp of sea salt

Instructions

Preheat oven to around 400 degrees F. Microwave cream cheese and mozzarella in a bowl. Add the rest of the ingredients and mix. Make the round crust by flattening the dough. Make holes and place them in a tray lined with parchment paper. Bake for around 12 minutes and mix rosemary, garlic, salt and butter in the bowl. Spread on bread and bake for another 10 minutes.

10 Parmesan chips

(Ready in about 10 minutes | Serving 2 | Difficulty: Easy)

Per serving: Kcal 263, Fat: 19g, Net Carbs: 2g, Protein: 17g

Ingredients

- 21/2 tbsp of pumpkin seeds
- 1 tbsp of chia seeds
- 3/4 cup of shredded cheese Parmesan
- 2 tbsp of whole flaxseed

Instructions

Preheat oven to around 350 degrees F. Line parchment paper on a baking sheet. Mix seeds and cheese in a bowl. Spoon mixture on a sheet in small mounds. Bake for around 10 minutes.

11 Low-carb bread

(Ready in about 30 minutes | Serving 4 | Difficulty: Easy)

Per serving: Kcal 311, Fat: 14g, Net Carbs: 2g, Protein: 6g

Ingredients

- 41/2 oz. of cream cheese
- 3 eggs
- 1 pinch of salt
- 1/2 tsp of baking powder
- 1/2 tbsp of psyllium husk ground
- 1/4 tsp of cream of tartar

Instructions

Separate whites and yolks in two bowls. Add salt to whites and mix. Mix cream cheese with yolks. Add husk powder and baking powder. Fold whites into yolk mixture. Line a baking tray with paper and add dollops of the mixture according to servings. Spread in the form of circles and bake for around 25 minutes at 300 degrees F.

12 Pizza crust

(Ready in about 35 minutes | Serving 4 | Difficulty: Moderate)

Per serving: Kcal 384, Fat: 31g, Net Carbs: 3g, Protein: 17g

Ingredients

- 11/4 cups of almond flour
- 1/4 cup of psyllium husk ground
- 1/4 cup of protein powder
- 2 tbsp of parmesan cheese grated
- 1/2 tsp of salt
- 11/2 oz. of melted butter
- 1 tbsp of Italian seasoning
- 2 eggs
- 2 tsp of baking powder
- 1 cup of boiling water
- olive oil

Instructions

Preheat oven to around 350 degrees F. Line parchment paper in two baking sheets and coat using oil. Mix dry ingredients in a bowl and stir eggs in it. Add boiling water and mix to form a thick dough. Divide in half and oil gently. Make two balls from the dough. Place on sheets and add parchment paper on the surface. Flatten balls with hands into thin crusts and discard paper. Bake for around 25 minutes. Take out and brush using coconut oil. Broil each side for around 3 minutes. Add toppings and bake for 10 more minutes at 425 degrees F.

13 Zucchini ciabatta

(Ready in about 25 minutes | Serving 4 | Difficulty: Hard)

Per serving: Kcal 409, Fat: 32g, Net Carbs: 7g, Protein: 17g

Ingredients

- 1 lb of zucchini
- 1 cup of almond flour
- sea salt
- 4 eggs
- 1/2 cup of sesame seeds
- 2 tbsp of psyllium husk ground
- 3 tbsp of sunflower seeds
- 1 tbsp of coconut flour
- 11/2 tsp of baking soda
- 1 tbsp of Italian seasoning
- 1/2 tsp of salt

Instructions

Preheat oven to around 400 degrees F. Rinse zucchini and shred finely. Squeeze extra liquid. Beat eggs in zucchini and mix dry ingredients in another bowl. Add to egg mixture and stir. Shape flat elongated pieces of bread and place on a parchment paper-lined baking sheet. Sprinkle sea salt and bake for around 20 minutes.

14 Keto dosa

(Ready in about 15 minutes | Serving 2 | Difficulty: Easy)

Per serving: Kcal 368, Fat: 33g, Net Carbs: 4g, Protein: 13g

Ingredients

- 1/2 cup of almond flour
- 1/2 tsp of coriander seed ground
- 1/2 cup of coconut milk
- 1/2 cup of shredded cheese mozzarella
- 1/2 tsp of ground cumin
- salt

Instructions

Mix everything in a bowl and warm oil in a pan. Pour batter and spread in the pan in a circular shape. Cook until cheese melts. Fold with a spatula once it is done.

15 Simple keto bread

(Ready in about 1 hour 10 minutes | Serving 6 | Difficulty: Hard)

Per serving: Kcal 311, Fat: 12g, Net Carbs: 2g, Protein: 6g

Ingredients

- 1/3 cup of psyllium husk ground
- 2 tbsp of sesame seeds
- 2 tsp of baking powder
- 11/4 cups of almond flour
- 1 tsp of sea salt
- 2 tsp of cider vinegar
- 1 cup of water
- 3 eggs, only whites

Instructions

Preheat oven to around 350 degrees F. Get a bowl to mix dry ingredients and boil water. Add egg whites and vinegar to the bowl and mix. Add boiling water and whisk into a thick dough. Make six rolls and place them on the baking sheet. Bake for around 60 minutes in the lower rack.

MidgetMomma.com

16 Seed crackers

(Ready in about 50 minutes | Serving 30 | Difficulty: Hard)

Per serving: Kcal 60, Fat: 6g, Net Carbs: 1g, Protein: 2g

Ingredients

- 1/3 cup of almond flour
- 1/3 cup of pumpkin seeds unsalted
- 1 tsp of salt
- 1/3 cup of flaxseed
- 1 cup of boiling water
- 1/3 cup of sesame seeds
- 1/3 cup of sunflower seeds unsalted
- 1 tbsp of psyllium husk ground
- 1/4 cup of coconut oil melted

Instructions

Preheat oven to around 300 degrees F. Add dry ingredients to a bowl and mix. Add oil and boiling water and form dough. Line parchment paper on the baking sheet and place dough. Add paper on top and flatten dough. Take the paper on top off and bake for around 45 minutes.

17 Sesame bread

(Ready in about 1 hour | Serving 30 | Difficulty: Hard)

Per serving: Kcal 61, Fat: 5g, Net Carbs: 1g, Protein: 2g

Ingredients

- 11/4 cups of sesame seeds
- 1/2 cup of cheddar cheese shredded
- 1/2 cup of sunflower seeds
- 1 tbsp of psyllium husk ground
- 2 eggs
- 1/2 cup of water
- 1/4 tsp of salt

Instructions

Preheat oven to around 350 degrees F. Line parchment paper in the baking sheet and mix everything in a bowl. Spread mixture on paper and sprinkle with salt. Bake for around 20 minutes. Take out and cut into the shape of your preference. Now bake for around 40 minutes at 275 degrees F.

18 Holiday bread

(Ready in about 1 hour | Serving 22 | Difficulty: Hard)

Per serving: Kcal 151, Fat: 12g, Net Carbs: 2g, Protein: 5g

Ingredients

- 2 cups of almond flour
- 1/3 cup of sesame seeds
- 1/2 cup of coconut flour
- 1 cup of sour cream
- 1/3 cup of flaxseed
- 1 tbsp of baking powder
- 1/4 cup of psyllium husk ground
- 3/4 tbsp of ground cloves
- 1/2 tbsp of fennel seeds
- 1/2 tbsp of orange peel ground
- 1 tsp of anise seeds
- 1 tsp of salt
- 1 tsp of ground cardamom
- 6 eggs
- 3 oz. of cream cheese

Instructions

Preheat the oven to 400 degrees F. Add dry ingredients to a bowl and mix. Mix cream cheese, eggs and sour cream in another bowl. Add to dry mixture and stir. Line a pan with parchment paper and pour the mixture on it. Bake for around 60 minutes.

19 Butter bread

(Ready in about 1 hour | Serving 20 | Difficulty: Hard)

Per serving: Kcal 91, Fat: 8g, Net Carbs: 1g, Protein: 2g

Ingredients

Bread

- 11/4 cups of almond flour
- 5 tbsp of psyllium husk ground
- 2 tsp of baking powder
- 1 tsp of sea salt
- 1 cup of water
- 2 tsp of cider vinegar
- 3 eggs, only whites

Garlic butter

- 4 oz. of butter
- 1 minced garlic clove
- 2 tbsp chopped fresh parsley
- 1/2 tsp of salt

Instructions

Preheat oven to around 350 degrees F. Line parchment paper on the baking sheet and mix dry ingredients in a bowl. Boil water and add egg whites, vinegar and water to dry ingredients. Whisk for around 30 seconds. Roll into hot dog-shaped buns and place them on a sheet. Bake for around 40 minutes. Mix ingredients for garlic butter and refrigerate. Cut buns from the center and spread butter. Bake for 15 minutes at 425 degrees F.

20 Bread twists

(Ready in about 25 minutes | Serving 10 | Difficulty: Easy)

Per serving: Kcal 181, Fat: 16g, Net Carbs: 1g, Protein: 7g

Ingredients

- 1/2 cup of almond flour
- 1/2 tsp of salt
- 1/4 cup of green pesto
- 1/4 cup of coconut flour
- 1 tsp of baking powder
- 2 oz. of butter
- 1 beaten egg
- 12/3 cups of shredded cheese mozzarella
- 1 beaten egg

Instructions

Preheat oven to around 350 degrees F. Add dry ingredients to a bowl and mix. Whisk eggs in a mixture and use a pot to melt cheese and butter. Add to bowl and make a firm dough by mixing. Place parchment paper and add dough to it. Form a rectangle with a rolling pin. Add pesto over dough and dice into strips(1 inch approx.). Twist and place on a parchment paper-lined baking sheet. Bake for around 20 minutes.

creationsbykara.com

21 French toast

(Ready in about 10 minutes | Serving 2 | Difficulty: Easy)

Per serving: Kcal 408, Fat: 37g, Net Carbs: 3g, Protein: 15g

Ingredients

Bread

- 2 tbsp of almond flour
- 2 tbsp of whipping cream
- 1 tsp of butter
- 2 tbsp of coconut flour
- 1 pinch of salt
- 11/2 tsp of baking powder
- 2 eggs

Batter

- 1 pinch of salt
- 2 tbsp of whipping cream
- 2 eggs
- 1/2 tsp of ground cinnamon
- 2 tbsp of butter

Instructions

Coat a glass dish with butter. Mix dry ingredients and break an egg. Stir and microwave for around 2 minutes. Take out of dish and dice in two pieces. Mix the rest of the ingredients in a bowl and pour on slices. Fry in butter and enjoy.

22 Soft tortillas

(Ready in about 20 minutes | Serving 6 | Difficulty: Easy)

Per serving: Kcal 236, Fat: 21g, Net Carbs: 1g, Protein: 5g

Ingredients

- 1/4 tsp of baking soda
- 11/2 cups of hot water
- 1 cup of coconut flour
- 1/2 tsp of salt
- 1/2 cup of avocado oil
- 1/4 cup of psyllium husk ground
- 3 egg whites

Instructions

Warm oil in a pan and mix baking soda, salt and coconut flour in a bowl. Whisk husk and drizzle oil. Fold in whites and add hot water, around 1/2 cup at once. Combine to form dough and shape into 12 balls. Place balls between parchment and flatten using a tortilla press. Toast each side for around 3 minutes.

23 Nut-free bread

(Ready in about 40 minutes | Serving 20 | Difficulty: Moderate)

Per serving: Kcal 109, Fat: 9g, Net Carbs: 1g, Protein: 6g

Ingredients

- 1 tbsp melted butter
- 6 eggs
- 1 oz. of cream cheese
- 3 cups of shredded cheese
- 2 tbsp of psyllium husk ground
- 1/2 cup of oat fiber
- 3 tsp of baking powder
- 1/2 tsp of salt

Topping

- 2 tbsp of poppy seeds
- 3 tbsp of sesame seeds

Instructions

Preheat oven to around 360 degrees F. Whisk eggs and add rest of ingredients in a bowl except butter. Coat a pan using butter and spread dough using a spatula. Sprinkle seeds on the dough and bake for around 35 minutes.

24 Fluffy bread

(Ready in about 1 hour 20 minutes | Serving 18 | Difficulty: Hard)

Per serving: Kcal 82, Fat: 7g, Net Carbs: 3g, Protein: 4g

Ingredients

- 1 cup of Almond Flour
- 1/3 cup of Butter
- 2 tsp of baking powder Gluten-free
- 1/4 cup of Coconut Flour
- 1/4 tsp of Sea salt
- 12 Egg whites

Instructions

Preheat oven to around 325 degrees F. Line parchment paper on a pan and add all the ingredients except tartar and eggs to the processor. Pulse and beat egg whites and tartar in a bowl using a hand mixer. Add half amount of whites to the processor and pulse. Transfer to bowl with rest of whites. Fold gently and place in pan. Bake for around 40 minutes. Bake for another 30 minutes after covering with foil.

25 90 Seconds Bread

(Ready in about 2 minutes | Serving 1 | Difficulty: Easy)

Per serving: Kcal 220, Fat: 21g, Net Carbs: 4g, Protein: 4g

Ingredients

- 1 tbsp of coconut flour
- 1 egg
- 1 tbsp of butter
- 1/2 tsp of baking powder double acting

Instructions

Add butter to a bowl and microwave. Mix the rest of the ingredients in butter and beat. Microwave for around 2 minutes and slice in two parts. Preheat oven to around 375 degrees F and bake for around 12 minutes.

26 Almond Flour Bread

(Ready in about 50 minutes | Serving 12 | Difficulty: Hard)

Per serving: Kcal 156, Fat: 14.2g, Net Carbs: 3.6g, Protein: 5.2g

Ingredients

- 2 whites of eggs
- pinch of salt
- 2 cups almond flour
- 2 eggs, yolks & whites
- 1/4 cup of butter melted
- 1 1/2 tsp of baking powder
- 4 tbsp of psyllium husks
- 1/2 tsp of xanthan gum
- 1/2 cup of warm water

Instructions

Preheat oven to around 350 degrees F. Break 2 eggs and 2 whites and beat. Add the rest of the ingredients and make a smooth dough by blending. Fill the baking tin and bake for around 45 minutes.

27 Plain Bread

(Ready in about 1 hour | Serving 12 | Difficulty: Hard)

Per serving: Kcal 247, Fat: 22.8g, Net Carbs: 4.9g, Protein: 7.7g

Ingredients

- 7 eggs
- cooking spray
- 1/2tsp of xanthan gum
- 1/2 cup melted butter
- 2 cups of almond flour blanched
- 2 tbsp of olive oil
- 1 tsp of baking powder
- 1/2tsp of sea salt

Instructions

Preheat oven to around 350 degrees F. Coat a pan using cooking spray and break and beat eggs in a bowl. Add butter and oil and mix. Mix the rest of the ingredients in another bowl. Add to eggs and mix. Pour in pan and bake for around 45 minutes.

veryEATalian.com

28 Fathead Bread

(Ready in about 55 minutes | Serving 4 | Difficulty: Hard)

Per serving: Kcal 240, Fat: 19.4g, Net Carbs: 4.2g, Protein: 13.5g

Ingredients

- 3/4 cup of shredded cheese mozzarella
- 1 egg
- 2 ounces of cream cheese
- 1/3 cup of almond flour
- 1/4tsp of garlic powder
- 2 tsp of baking powder
- 1/2 cup of shredded cheese Cheddar

Instructions

Microwave cream cheese and mozzarella in a bowl for around 20 seconds. Beat eggs in a bowl and add the rest of the ingredients. Add mozzarella mixture and mix. Transfer to plastic wrap and wrap over dough. Form a ball and place it in the fridge for around 30 minutes. Preheat oven to around 425 degrees F and oil a parchment paper-lined baking sheet. Take the dough out and remove the wrap. Make 4 pieces and roll each into the shape of a ball. Cut in half and place on sheet. Bake for around 12 minutes.

29 Bread Rolls

(Ready in about 1 hour 5 minutes | Serving 8 | Difficulty: Hard)

Per serving: Kcal 166, Fat: 12g, Net Carbs: 10g, Protein: 6.8g

Ingredients

- cooking spray
- 5 tbsp of psyllium husk
- 2 tbsp of sesame seeds
- 1 1/2 cups of almond flour blanched
- 1 tsp of sea salt
- 3 eggs, only whites
- 1 cup of boiling water
- 2 tsp of white vinegar

Instructions

Preheat oven to around 350 degrees F. Oil a baking sheet using cooking spray. Add the rest of the ingredients to a bowl and mix using an electric mixer to form a dough. Make 8 rolls from the dough and place them on a sheet. Sprinkle seeds and bake for around 55 minutes.

30 Simple and Easy Bread

(Ready in about 1 hour 10 minutes | Serving 1 | Difficulty: Hard)

Per serving: Kcal 450, Fat: 40g, Net Carbs: 10g, Protein: 19g

Ingredients

- 6 eggs
- 1 tbsp of baking powder
- 1/4 cup of melted butter
- 1/2 tsp of cream of tartar
- 1 1/2 cup of finely ground almond flour
- 1/2 tsp of kosher salt

Instructions

Preheat oven to around 375 degrees F. Line parchment paper in a pan and separate egg yolks and whites. Combine whites with tartar in a bowl and beat yolk with the rest of the ingredients in another bowl. Fold in whites and transfer to pan. Bake for around 30 minutes.

31 Gluten-free Bread

(Ready in about 1 hour 15 minutes | Serving 10 | Difficulty: Hard)

Per serving: Kcal 53, Fat: 3g, Net Carbs: 4g, Protein: 2g

Ingredients

- 1 1/4 cups of almond flour
- 2 tbsp of sesame seeds
- 2 tsp of baking powder
- 5 tbsp of psyllium husk ground
- 1 tsp of salt
- 1 cup of boiling water
- 2 tsp of apple cider vinegar
- 3 eggs, only whites

Instructions

Preheat oven to around 350 degrees F. Line parchment paper in loaf tin after coating with butter. Combine husk, salt, almond flour and baking powder in a bowl. Add cider vinegar and egg whites to dry ingredients and mix using an electric mixer. Add boiling water slowly and mix. A dough will form. Transfer to the tin and sprinkle seeds. Bake for around 60 minutes.

32 Collagen Bread

(Ready in about 1 hour 50 minutes | Serving 12 | Difficulty: Hard)

Per serving: Kcal 311, Fat: 5g, Net Carbs: 1g, Protein: 7g

Ingredients

- 1/2 cup of Collagen Protein Grass-Fed
- 1 tsp of xanthan gum
- 6 tbsp of almond flour
- 5 separated eggs, pastured
- 1 tbsp of coconut oil unflavored
- 1 tsp of baking powder aluminum-free
- Pinch of Himalayan salt

Instructions

Preheat oven to around 325 degrees F. Oil a loaf dish and beat egg whites in a bowl. Mix dry ingredients in another bowl. Mix yolks, coconut oil and wet ingredients in another bowl. Add both mixtures to whites and beat. Pour into the dish and bake for around 40 minutes.

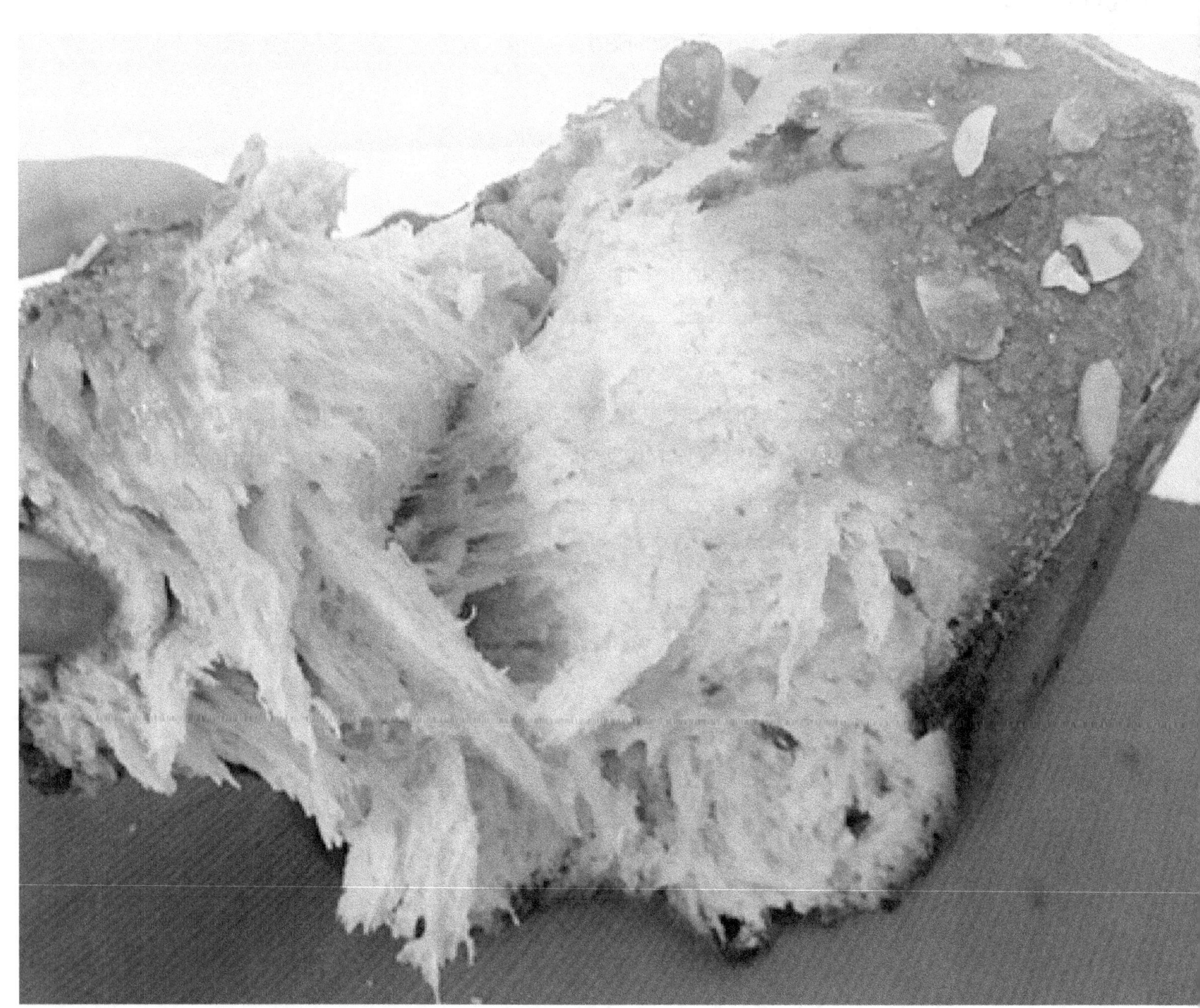

33 Coconut Bread

(Ready in about 1 hour 10 minutes | Serving 10 | Difficulty: Hard)

Per serving: Kcal 318, Fat: 17g, Net Carbs: 9g, Protein: 12g

Ingredients

- 1/2 cup coconut flour
- 1/4 cup of coconut oil
- 1/4 tsp of baking soda
- 1/4 tsp of salt
- 6 eggs
- 1/4 of almond milk unsweetened

Instructions

Preheat your oven to around 350 degrees F. Line parchment paper in a pan and combine salt, soda and coconut flour in a bowl. Mix oil, milk and eggs in another bowl. Incorporate both mixtures and pour in pan. Bake for around 50 minutes.

34 Macadamia Bread

(Ready in about 35 minutes | Serving 10 | Difficulty: Moderate)

Per serving: Kcal 151, Fat: 14g, Net Carbs: 4g, Protein: 5g

Ingredients

- 5 oz of macadamia nuts
- 1/2 tsp of apple cider vinegar
- 1/4 cup of coconut flour
- 5 eggs
- 1/2 tsp of baking soda

Instructions

Preheat oven to around 350 degrees F. Pulse nuts in processor and add eggs, and pulse again. Add rest of ingredients and pulse to incorporate thoroughly. Oil a pan and pour the mixture, and bake for around 40 minutes.

35 Cauliflower Bread

(Ready in about 1 hour 18 minutes | Serving 6 | Difficulty: Hard)

Per serving: Kcal 108, Fat: 8g, Net Carbs: 8g, Protein: 6g

Ingredients

- 3 cups of riced cauliflower
- 1 tbsp chopped fresh rosemary
- 1 1/4 cup of Coconut Flour Wholesome
- 10 separated Egg
- 1 1/2 tbsp of baking powder Gluten-free
- 1 tbsp chopped fresh parsley

Instructions

Preheat oven to around 350 degrees F. Line parchment paper in a pan and steam cauliflower in the microwave until it is soft. Beat egg whites and tartar in a bowl with a mixer. Add the rest of the ingredients with a quarter of whites in the processor. Squeeze cauliflower in a kitchen towel to dry it. Add to blender and pulse. Add rest of whites and pulse. Fold in the rosemary and parsley. Transfer to pan and bake for around 50 minutes.

36 Keto Tortillas

(Ready in about 15 minutes | Serving 8 | Difficulty: Easy)

Per serving: Kcal 89, Fat: 6g, Net Carbs: 4g, Protein: 3g

Ingredients

- 96 g of almond flour
- 3 tsp of water
- 2 tsp of xanthan gum
- 24 g of coconut flour
- 1 tsp of baking powder
- 2 tsp of apple cider vinegar
- 1/4 tsp of kosher salt
- 1 beaten egg

Instructions

Break eggs in a bowl and whisk. Add rest of ingredients except cider vinegar in processor and blend. Add cider vinegar while the blender is running. Once it is uniformly distributed, add eggs and water. Once a ball forms from the dough, stop. Wrap using cling film and through plastic, knead for around 1 minute. Warm a pan and form eight balls of 1 inch. Roll out balls in two parchment papers. Place in pan and cook for around 6 seconds. Flip and cook until each side is a bit golden.

37 Buttery Flatbread

(Ready in about 7 minutes | Serving 2 | Difficulty: Easy)

Per serving: Kcal 232, Fat: 19g, Net Carbs: 9g, Protein: 9g

Ingredients

- 1 cup of Almond Flour
- 1 tbsp of Oil
- 2 tsp of Xanthan Gum
- 2 tbsp of Coconut Flour
- 1/2 tsp of Baking Powder
- 1 Egg plus 1 Egg White
- 1/2 tsp of Falk Salt
- 1 tbsp of Water
- 1 tbsp of melted Butter

Instructions

Mix dry ingredients in a bowl. Add eggs to flour and mix. Add water and work with dough, so moisture is absorbed. Make 4 parts of dough and press using cling wrap. Warm oil in the pan and fry each side of bread for around 1 minute. Brush butter on top and garnish using parsley and salt.

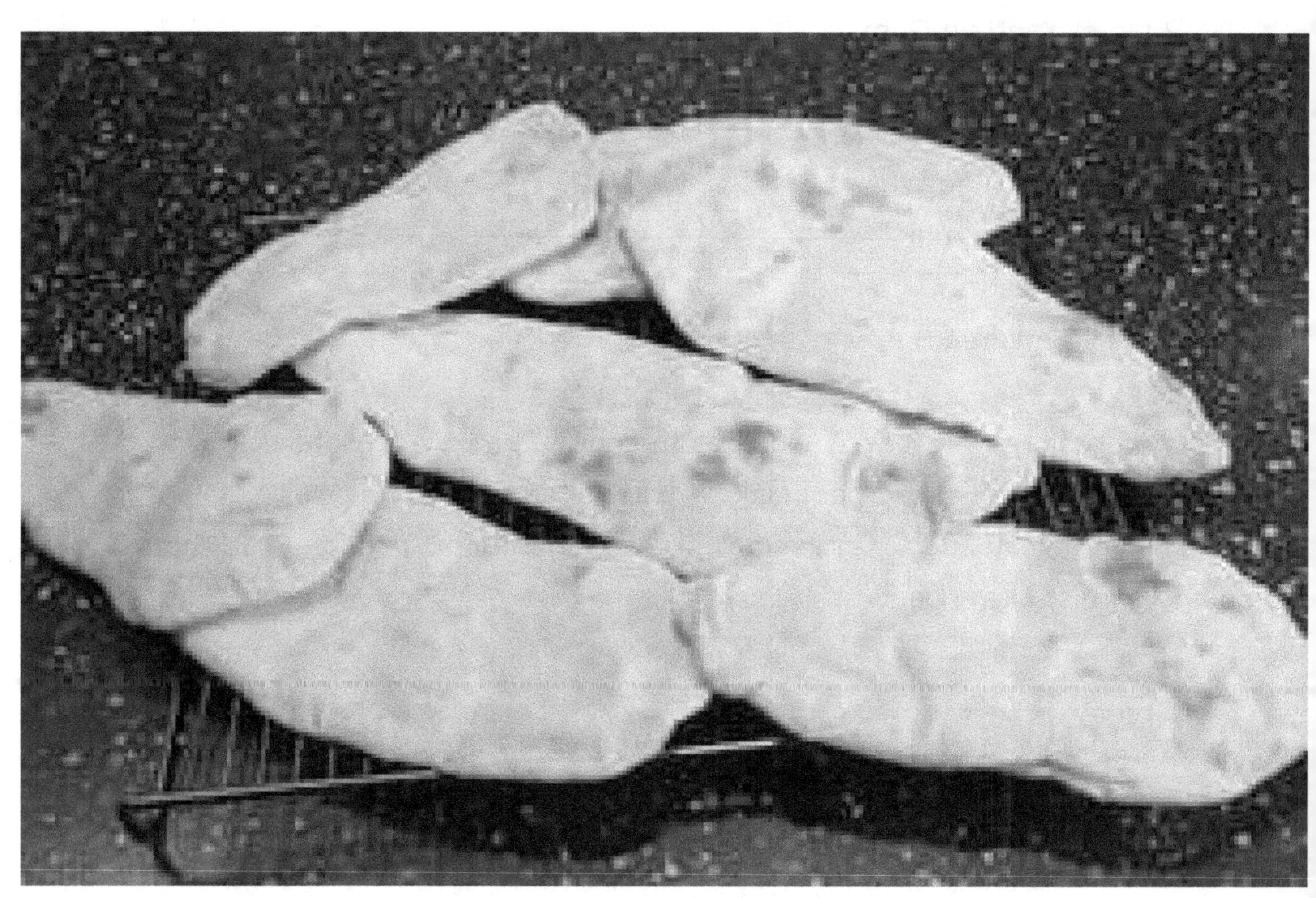

38 Gluten-Free Biscuits

(Ready in about 30 minutes | Serving 6 | Difficulty: Easy)

Per serving: Kcal 290, Fat: 30g, Net Carbs: 8g, Protein: 7g

Ingredients

- 1 egg
- 2 tsp. of apple vinegar
- 77 g of sour cream
- 2 tbsp of water
- 96 g of almond flour
- 1 tbsp of apple cider vinegar
- 63 g of flaxseed meal golden
- 20 g of whey protein
- 21 g of coconut flour
- 3 1/2 tsp of baking powder
- 1/2 tsp of kosher salt
- 1 tsp of xanthan gum
- 112 g of organic butter grass-fed

Instructions

Preheat your oven to around 450 degrees F. Line parchment paper in a tray. Mix eggs, water, apple vinegar and sour cream in a bowl. Add rest of ingredients except butter in blender and pulse. Add butter and blend again. Pour bowl mixture and blend until incorporated. Make 6 rounds from dough and place in the tray. Brush butter and place in oven. Bake for around 20 minutes.

39 Cauliflower Buns

(Ready in about 45 minutes | Serving 6 | Difficulty: Hard)

Per serving: Kcal 43, Fat: 1.9g, Net Carbs: 3.5g, Protein: 3.3g

Ingredients

- 2 cups of cauliflower rice
- 2 tbsp of coconut flour
- 2 beaten eggs
- 1/4 tsp of ground turmeric
- 1/4 tsp of black pepper ground
- 1/2 tsp of sea salt

Instructions

Preheat your oven to around 400 degrees F. Line parchment paper on the baking sheet. Mix everything in a bowl and make six buns from the batter. Place on sheet and bake for around 30 minutes.

40 Low Carb Biscuits

(Ready in about 25 minutes | Serving 12 | Difficulty: Easy)

Per serving: Kcal 164, Fat: 15g, Net Carbs: 4g, Protein: 5g

Ingredients

- 1/3 cup of Butter
- 2 cups of Blanched Wholesome Yum Almond Flour
- 1/2 tsp of Sea salt
- 2 tsp of baking powder Gluten-free
- 2 whisked egg

Instructions

Preheat oven to around 350 degrees F. Line parchment paper on the baking sheet. Add all the ingredients to a bowl and whisk. Scoop on the sheet in the amount of tbsp. Form biscuit shapes and bake for around 15 minutes.

41 Pizza Crust

(Ready in about 10 minutes | Serving 4| Difficulty: Easy)

Per serving: Kcal 125, Fat: 10g, Net Carbs: 6g, Protein: 8g

Ingredients

- 1 tbsp of coconut flour
- 8 egg whites
- 1/2 tsp of baking powder
- 1/4 cup of sifted coconut flour
- Pepper, salt and Italian spices

Pizza sauce

- 1 tsp of dried basil
- 2 cloves of garlic crushed
- 1/2 cup of tomato sauce
- 1/4 tsp of sea salt

Instructions

Whisk egg in a bowl and add coconut flour. Whisk and add mixed spices and baking powder and keep whisking until fully incorporated. Warm a pan after oiling it lightly. Pour mixture into the pan and cook for around 4 minutes. Flip and cook for 2 more minutes. Dust with coconut flour. Combine sauce ingredients in a bowl and spread on crust.

42 Zucchini Bread

(Ready in about 1 hour 20 minutes | Serving 16 | Difficulty: Hard)

Per serving: Kcal 200, Fat: 17g, Net Carbs: 2.6g, Protein: 6g

Ingredients

- 3 eggs
- 1 tsp of vanilla extract
- 1/2cup of olive oil
- 2 1/2cups of almond flour
- 1 cup of grated zucchini
- 1/2tsp of salt
- 1 1/2 cups of erythritol
- 1 1/2tsp of baking powder
- 1 tsp of ground cinnamon
- 1/2tsp of nutmeg
- 1/4tsp of ground ginger
- 1/2cup of chopped walnuts

Instructions

Preheat your oven to around 350 degrees F. Mix oil, eggs and vanilla in a bowl. Mix erythritol, baking powder, salt, nutmeg, almond flour, ginger and cinnamon in another bowl. Squeeze zucchini in a paper towel and add to eggs. Add dry ingredients to the egg and blend. Spray a pan using cooking spray and spoon mixture. Add walnuts and press with a spatula. Bake for around 70 minutes.

43 Blueberry Muffin Bread

(Ready in about 1 hour | Serving 12 | Difficulty: Hard)

Per serving: Kcal 156, Fat: 13g, Net Carbs: 4g, Protein: 5g

Ingredients

- 1/4 cup of butter
- 1/2 cup of almond butter
- 5 eggs
- 1/2 cup of almond flour
- 2 tsp of baking powder
- 1/2 tsp of salt
- 1/2 cup of almond milk
- 1/2 cup of blueberries

Instructions

Preheat the oven to around 350 degrees F. Melt butter and nut butter in a bowl and stir. Mix baking powder, salt and almond flour in another bowl and pour butter mixture. Stir and take another bowl to mix eggs and almond milk. Pour in flour and butter mixture and stir. Add blueberries and stir. Line parchment paper in the pan and oil it. Pour batter and bake for around 45 minutes.

44 Cranberry Bread

(Ready in about 1 hour 25 minutes | Serving 12 | Difficulty: Hard)

Per serving: Kcal 175, Fat: 14g, Net Carbs: 8g, Protein: 7g

Ingredients

- 1 1/2 cups of almond flour
- 1/2 cup of white sweetener
- 1/2 cup of almond milk unsweetened
- 1/2 cup of coconut flour
- 1/2tsp of 30% extract monk fruit
- 1 1/2tsp of baking powder
- 1 tbsp of orange peel dried
- 1/2tsp of baking soda
- 1/2tsp of ground cinnamon
- 1/2tsp of xanthan gum
- 1/2tsp of salt
- 1/4 cup of butter melted unsalted
- 1/4tsp of ground nutmeg
- 6 eggs
- 6 ounces of cranberries

Instructions

Preheat oven to around 325 degrees F. Oil a pan and line using parchment paper. Mix everything except butter, egg and almond milk in a bowl. Mix them in a separate bowl. Add to dry ingredients and whisk. Fold the mixture in cranberries and pour in a pan. Bake for around 1 hour.

45 Fluffy Buns

(Ready in about 30 minutes | Serving 4 | Difficulty: Easy)

Per serving: Kcal 109, Fat: 12.5g, Net Carbs: 2.3g, Protein: 7.3g

Ingredients

- 1 egg
- 1 tsp of baking powder
- 3 eggs, only whites
- 1/4 cup of hot water
- 1/4 cup of coconut flour
- 1/4 cup of almond flour
- 1 tbsp of psyllium husk ground
- Sesame seeds

Instructions

Preheat oven to around 356 F and mix dry ingredients in a bowl. Add everything to the blender and blend for around 20 seconds. Make four portions from dough and shape buns. Place on sheet and sprinkle seeds on top. Bake for around 25 minutes.

Cooking
from
Heart

46 Ultimate Buns

(Ready in about 1 hour | Serving 1 | Difficulty: Hard)

Per serving: Kcal 208, Fat: 15.2g, Net Carbs: 4.2g, Protein: 10.1g

Dry ingredients

- 2/3 cup of psyllium husks ground
- 1 1/2 cup of almond flour
- 1/2 cup of coconut flour
- 5 tbsp of sesame seeds2 tsp of garlic powder
- 1/2 cup of flax meal
- 2 tsp of onion powder
- 1 tsp of baking soda
- 2 tsp of cream of tartar
- 1 tsp of Himalayan salt

Wet ingredients

- 2 eggs
- 6 egg whites
- 2 cups of water

Instructions

Preheat oven to around 350 degrees F. Add dry ingredients except for sesame seeds and mix. Add eggs and mix. Make buns with a spoon. Line a tray using parchment paper and place buns. Top with seeds and bake for around 55 minutes.

47 Dinner Rolls

(Ready in about 15 minutes | Serving 6 | Difficulty: Easy)

Per serving: Kcal 219, Fat: 18g, Net Carbs: 5.6g, Protein: 16g10.7g

Ingredients

- 1 Cup of Mozzarella, shredded
- 1 Cup of Almond Flour
- 1 oz of Cream Cheese
- 1/4 Cup of Flax Seed Ground
- 1/2 Tsp of Baking Soda
- 1 egg

Instructions

Preheat the oven to around 400 degrees F. Line parchment paper on the baking sheet. Microwave mozzarella and cream cheese in a bowl. Stir and add eggs. Combine baking soda, flax and almond flour in another bowl. Add egg mixture and cheese to this mixture. Make 6 balls from the dough. Place on sheet and bake for around 12 minutes.

48 Bagel Scones

(Ready in about 40 minutes | Serving 12 | Difficulty: Moderate)

Per serving: Kcal 161, Fat: 13.5g, Net Carbs: 6.5g, Protein: 5.7g

Ingredients

- 2 cups of almond flour
- 1 tbsp of baking powder
- 1/4 cup of coconut flour
- 1/2 tsp of garlic powder
- 2 eggs
- 1/4 tsp of salt
- 1/4 cup of whipping cream
- 2 tbsp of Bagel Seasoning
- 1 tbsp of butter melted

Instructions

Preheat the oven to around 325 degrees F. Line parchment paper on the baking sheet and oil it gently. Mix everything except bagel seasoning, whipping cream and egg in a bowl. Then stir whipping cream and egg until you get a dough. Place on sheet and shape into a rectangle roughly. Make 6 squares with a knife and cut diagonally each to make two triangles. Sprinkle with bagel seasoning and bake for around 25 minutes.

49 Avocado bread

(Ready in about 1 hour 35 minutes | Serving 9 | Difficulty: Hard)

Per serving: Kcal 214, Fat: 19.1g, Net Carbs: 4.5g, Protein: 10.3g

Ingredients

- 1 cup of almond flour
- 2 tbsp of Swerve Sweetener
- 1/3 cup of whey protein
- 2 tsp of baking powder
- 3 eggs, separated
- 1/2 tsp of salt
- 1 large egg
- 2 tbsp of water
- 3 tbsp of avocado oil
- 1/2 tsp of cream of tartar

Instructions

Preheat oven to around 325 degrees F and line parchment paper in the pan. Mix dry ingredients in one bowl and wet ingredients except tartar and whites in a separate bowl. Add egg mixture to dry ingredients and whisk to combine. Beat whites and tartar in another bowl and fold whites in the batter. Pour batter into the pan and cook for around 50 minutes.

50 Croissants

(Ready in about 50 minutes | Serving 8 | Difficulty: Hard)

Per serving: Kcal 141, Fat: 9.6g, Net Carbs: 4.6g, Protein: 8.4g

Ingredients

- 1 tbsp melted butter
- 1/4 cup of coconut flour
- 1/2 tsp of xanthan gum
- 2 tbsp of Sweetener
- 1 tsp of baking powder
- 1 egg
- 6 ounces of mozzarella
- 1/3 tbsp of almond paste
- 1 tbsp of sliced almonds

Instructions

Preheat oven to around 400 degrees F. Line a baking sheet and whisk coconut flour, xantham gum, baking powder and sweetener in a bowl. Melt cheese in the microwave for around 30 seconds. Knead after stirring in the egg and flour mixture in the bowl with a spatula. Pour on the sheet and cover with parchment paper. Roll into a circle of 12 inches. Take 1.5 tbsp of almond paste and shape a thin log of length around 3 inches. Position at the wide end of 1 wedge and fold the dough around almond paste tightly. Pinch to seal and repeat with the rest of the dough. Curve ends of dough to make a crescent shape. Add sliced almonds and bake for around 25 minutes after turning the temperature to 350 degrees F. Dust using sweetener.

51 Gluten-Free Bagels

(Ready in about 30 minutes | Serving 6 | Difficulty: Easy)

Per serving: Kcal 364, Fat: 27.9g, Sodium 919.8mg, Protein: 20.9g

Ingredients

- 1 tbsp. baking powder, gluten-free
- 1 ½ cups of almond flour
- 2 eggs
- 1 tsp. garlic salt
- 2 oz. cream cheese, cubed
- 2 ½ cups of shredded mozzarella cheese

Instructions

- Preheat oven to 400 degrees Fahrenheit. Using parchment paper, line the baking sheet.
- In a mixing bowl, add the baking powder, garlic salt, and almond flour.
- In the microwave-safe bowl, mix mozzarella and cream cheese. Microwave for one minute, then remove and mix. Microwave for another minute, then take it off and stir until all is well combined. Working fast, stir the eggs and flour mixture into melted cheese mixture. Knead the dough by hand until it becomes a sticky dough. Continue kneading and pressing the dough for approximately two minutes or until it is fully uniform.
- The dough can be divided into six equal bits. Roll each one into the long log, then push the ends together to form a bagel shape and put it on the baking sheet that has been prepared.
- For ten to fourteen minutes in the preheated oven, bake till the bagels are golden.

52 Fluffy Keto Pancakes

(Ready in about 10 minutes | Serving 4 | Difficulty: Easy)
Per serving: Kcal 383, Fat: 32.2g, Sodium 842.3mg, Protein: 15.3g

Ingredients

- ¼ cup of coconut flour
- 1 cup of almond flour
- 2 tbsp. natural sweetener, low-calorie
- 1 tsp. baking powder
- 1 tsp. salt
- ½ tsp. ground cinnamon
- ¼ cup of heavy whipping cream, at room temp.
- 6 eggs, at room temp.
- 1 tsp. vanilla extract
- 2 tbsp. melted butter

Directions

- In a mixing bowl, add coconut flour, almond flour, salt, sweetener, cinnamon, and baking powder. Slowly whisk in the heavy cream, eggs, vanilla extract, and butter till just mixed.
- Over medium-high flame, gently oil a griddle. Cook till the bubbles form and the sides are dry, three to four minutes, by dropping batter by big spoonfuls onto griddle. Cook for two or three minutes on the other hand, until browned. Continue with the remaining batter.
- Cholesterol 281.2mg

53 High Protein Bread

(Ready in about 2hrs 40 mins | Serving 10 | Difficulty: Medium)

Per serving: Kcal 137, Fat: 2.4g, Sodium 235mg, Protein: 6.5g

Ingredients

- 2 tsp dry yeast active
- 1 cup of bread flour
- 1 cup of flour whole wheat
- ¼ cup of soy flour
- ¼ cup of soymilk powder
- ¼ cup of oat bran
- 1 tbsp of canola oil
- 1 tbsp of honey
- 1 tsp of salt
- 1 cup of water

Directions

In the bread machine pan, arrange the ingredients in an order prescribed by the maker. Choose between the standard medium and regular settings; click Start.

Conclusion

A keto diet may be a healthier option for certain people, although the amount of fat, carbohydrates, and protein prescribed varies from person to person. If you have diabetes, talk to the doctor before starting the diet because it would almost certainly need prescription changes and stronger blood sugar regulation. Are you taking drugs for high blood pressure? Before starting a keto diet again, talk to the doctor. If you're breastfeeding, you shouldn't follow a ketogenic diet. Be mindful that limiting carbs will render you irritable, hungry, and sleepy, among other things. However, this may be a one-time occurrence. Keep in mind that you can eat a balanced diet in order to obtain all of the vitamins and minerals you need. A sufficient amount of fiber is also needed. When the body begins to derive energy from accumulated fat rather than glucose, it is said to be in ketosis. Several trials have shown the powerful weight-loss benefits of a low-carb, or keto, diet. This diet, on the other hand, can be difficult to stick to and can exacerbate health issues in individuals who have certain disorders, such as diabetes type 1. The keto diet is suitable for the majority of citizens. Nonetheless, all major dietary modifications should be discussed with a dietitian or doctor. This is essentially the case with people who have inherent conditions. The keto diet may be an effective therapy for people with drug-resistant epilepsy. Though the diet may be beneficial to people of any age, teenagers, people over 50, and babies can profit the most because they can easily stick to it. Modified keto diets, such as the revised Atkins diet or the low-glycemic index diet, are safer for adolescents and adults. A health care worker should keep a careful eye on someone who is taking a keto diet as a treatment. A doctor and dietitian will maintain track of a person's progress, administer drugs, and test for side effects. The body absorbs fat and protein differently than it does carbohydrates. Carbohydrates have a high insulin reaction. The protein sensitivity to insulin is mild, and the quick insulin response is negligible. Insulin is a fat-producing and fat-conserving enzyme. If you wish to lose weight, consume as many eggs, chickens, fish, and birds as you want, satiate yourself with the fat, and then eat every vegetable that grows on the ground. Butter and coconut oil can be used instead of processed synthetic seed oils. You may be either a sugar or a fat burner, but not both.

Keto Chaffle Cookbook

The Best Keto Guide With Easy And Tasty low Carb and Gluten Free Keto Chaffle Recipes To start Off Your Day

By

Emily Baker

Introduction

Ketogenic refers to a low-carbohydrate diet. The aim is to eat more calories from fat and protein while eating fewer calories from carbohydrates. The carbohydrates that are easiest to digest, such as starch, pastries, soda, and white bread, are the first to go. When you consume fewer than 50 g of carbohydrates a day, your body easily runs out of energy. This normally takes three or four days. Then you'll begin to break down fat and protein for energy, potentially resulting in weight loss. Ketosis is the term for this state. It's crucial to remember that the ketogenic diet is a short-term diet designed to help you lose weight rather than change your lifestyle. A ketogenic diet is more often used to reduce weight, although it may also be used to treat medical problems such as epilepsy. It can even benefit those suffering from heart failure, some brain disorders, and even acne, although further study is required. Since the keto diet contains too much fat, adherents must ingest fat at every meal time. In a normal 2K-calorie diet, that would seem like 165 g of fat, 40 g of carbohydrates, and 75 g of protein. The exact ratio, on the other hand, is determined by your basic requirements. Nuts (walnuts, almonds), avocados, seeds, olive oil and tofu are among the healthier unsaturated fats allowed on the keto diet. However, oils (coconut, palm), butter, lard, and peanut butter all contain high amounts of saturated fats. Protein is an essential aspect of the keto diet, although it is also difficult to discern between protein items that are lean and protein products rich in fat(saturated), such as beef, bacon, and pork. What for fruits and vegetables? While fruits are generally rich in carbohydrates, unique fruits may be obtained in limited quantities (generally berries) Leafy greens (like kale, chard, Swiss chard, and spinach), broccoli, cauliflower, asparagus, tomatoes, brussels sprouts, bell peppers, garlic, cucumbers, mushrooms, summer squashes, as well as celery are also rich in carbohydrates. One cup of sliced broccoli includes about six carbohydrates. At the same time, there are several possible keto hazards, such as liver deficiency, liver complications, constipation, kidney disorders, and so on. As a result, we can also keep our Keto diet portions in check.

Understanding The Ketogenic Diet

This chapter delves into the Ketogenic diet in depth. The chapter further discusses which foods to consume on the Keto diet and which foods to stop while on this diet. The Keto diet is often explained in-depth, including how it functions and what health advantages it provides.

The ketogenic diet (or keto diet) is a high-fat, low-carbohydrate diet with various health benefits. Evidently, more than 20 studies suggest that this form of diet will help you lose weight and boost your wellbeing. Diabetes patients, epilepsy patients, patients suffering from Alzheimer's disease, as well as cancer can all benefit from ketogenic diets.

1.1 What is Keto?

The ketogenic diet is a very low carbohydrate, high-fat diet that has a lot in common with the Atkins diet and other low-carb diets. It necessitates a significant reduction of carbohydrate consumption and a replacement with fat. This reduction of carbohydrates puts the body into a metabolic condition known as ketosis. As this occurs, the body's energy production of fat-burning skyrockets. In addition, it converts fat into ketones in the liver, which will supply energy to the brain. Ketogenic diets can result in substantial reductions in insulin as well as blood sugar levels. This, along with the increased ketones, has numerous health benefits.

Ketogenic Diets Come in Many Forms

There are a few variations of the ketogenic diet, including:

The traditional ketogenic diet consists of a diet that is low in carbs, mild in protein, and strong in fats. It usually has a 75 percent fat content, a 5% carbohydrate content, and a 20% protein content.

The cyclic ketogenic diet entails high-carb reefed cycles, such as five ketogenic days accompanied by two days of high carbohydrate use.

A ketogenic diet with particular goals: The diet requires carbs to be inserted in between exercises.

Protein-rich ketogenic diet: This is comparable to a normal keto diet, but it contains extra protein. Usually, the ratio is 60 percent fat, 5% sugars, and 35 percent protein. However, only normal and protein-rich ketogenic diets have been extensively studied. More complex keto diets, such as targeted or cyclic keto, are mainly utilized by bodybuilders and athletes.

Ketogenic Diet Health Benefits

In fact, the keto diet first gained popularity as a means of treating neurological conditions, such as epilepsy. Following that, research has shown that diet can help with a broad variety of health issues:

Heart disease: The keto diet has been found to decrease risk factors such as body fat, blood sugar, HDL cholesterol and blood pressure.

Alzheimer's disease: The ketogenic diet can ease Alzheimer's symptoms while still delaying the disease's progression.

Epilepsy: Research has demonstrated that a ketogenic diet can significantly reduce seizures in children with epileptic seizures.

Cancer: The diet is actually being used to control a number of diseases and to delay tumor development.

Acne: Lower insulin levels, as well as less sugar or fried food diets, will aid acne recovery.

Parkinson's disease: According to one report, diet can help relieve the effects of Parkinson's disease.

Brain injuries: One study found that the diet would also increase concussions and improve recovery after a brain injury.

Polycystic ovary syndrome: A ketogenic diet may help lower insulin levels and can be helpful in the treatment of polycystic ovary syndrome.

What foods can you consume on a ketogenic diet?

The majority of your meals will revolve around the following foods:

- Salmon, mackerel and tuna are representations of fatty fish.
- Look for pastured eggs, whole eggs, or omega-3 eggs.
- Seek for grass-fed butter plus cream wherever possible.
- Red meat, ham, sausage, turkey, bacon, chicken and steak are all examples of meat.
- Non-processed cheese (goat, cheddar, mozzarella, blue, or cream).
- Flax seeds, walnuts, almonds, pumpkin seeds, chia seeds and other nuts and beans
- Avocado oil, olive oil and coconut oil are the other safe oils.
- Salt, spices and pepper, as well as a variety of herbs, may be used as condiments.
- Avocados: entire avocados or guacamole made freshly.
- Low-carb vegetables including greens, tomatoes, onions, peppers and other related veggies.

Foods to avoid on a ketogenic diet include:

Carbohydrate-rich diets can be avoided as much as possible.

The following is a selection of items that must be eliminated or reduced on a ketogenic diet:

- Sugary drink, ice cream, soda, smoothies, cake, candy and other sugary items
- Wheat, pasta, cereals, rice, and other wheat-based products are examples of starches or grains.
- Sweet potatoes, parsnips, parsnips, potatoes, carrots and other tubers & root vegetables
- Reduced-calorie or low-fat foods are extremely processed and abundant in carbohydrates.
- Fruit: All fruits, with the exception of tiny bits of berries like strawberries.
- Chickpeas, lentils, peas, kidney beans, and other legumes or beans
- Some sauces/condiments: They are also high in unhealthy fat and sugar.
- Unhealthy fats: Limit the intake to mayonnaise, processed vegetable oils, and other processed fats.

- Alcohol: Because of their carb content, certain alcoholic beverages will shake you out of ketosis.
- Dietary ingredients that are sugar-free: Alcohols, which are often rich in sugar, may influence ketone levels in certain situations. These objects seem to have passed through a lot of refining as well.

1.2 What is the Keto diet, and how does it work?

The "ketogenic" keto diet consists of consuming a moderate level of protein, a heavy amount of fat, and relatively little carbohydrates; also, the fruit is forbidden. As for every diet fad, the advantages to adherents include improved vitality, weight reduction, and mental clarity. Is the ketogenic diet, though, what it's cracked up to be?

Dietitians and nutritionists are quiet on the topic. Low-carb diets like keto appear to assist with weight loss in the short term, but they are no more successful than any other self-help or conventional diet. They still don't seem to be enhancing athletic results.

The ketogenic diet was created to treat epilepsy instead of losing weight. In the 1920s, physicians found that holding people on low-carb diets induced their bodies to use fat as the predominant fuel source rather than glucose. When only fat is available for the body to combust or burn, the body converts fats to fatty acids, which are then converted to ketones, which can be used and taken up to power the body's cells.

Currently, feeding the body exclusively ketones prevents epilepsy for unclear causes. However, with the advent of anti-seizure medicines, few patients with epilepsy rely on ketogenic diets anymore, while certain people who may not respond to medications may benefit. Low carb diets like the Atkins diet, which gained popularity in the early 2000s, also spawned keto diets for weight loss. In comparison, all groups of meatier-meal diets restrict carbohydrates. This diet does not have a set structure, although most routines provide for fewer than fifty grams of carbs per day.

A keto diet causes the body to enter a state known as ketosis, in which the body's cells become completely reliant on ketones for nutrition. It's not exactly clear that this leads to weight loss, but ketosis decreases appetite and can affect hunger-controlling hormones, including insulin. As a consequence, proteins and fats can keep humans fuller longer than sugars, resulting in lower net calorie intake.

In one head-to-head comparison, researchers looked at 48 separate diet trials in which subjects were randomly allocated to one of the well-known diets. Low-carb diets like South Beach, Atkins, and Zone, as well as low-fat diets like Ornish diets and portion restriction diets like Weight Watchers and Jenny Craig, were among the options.

Every diet resulted in greater weight loss than almost no diet after six months, according to the results. Low-carb and low-fat dieters lost almost equal amounts of weight as compared to non-dieters, with low-carb dieters losing 19 pounds on average versus low-fat dieters dropping 17.6 pounds (7.99 kilograms). At 12 months, both diet styles displayed symptoms of dropping off, with low-fat and low-carb dieters being 16 pounds (7.27 kg) smaller on average than non-dieters.

There were few differences in weight reduction within the diets of designated people. This is in line with the practice of recommending every diet that an individual practice in order to lose weight.

Another study of well-known diets discovered the Atkins diet, which results in greater weight loss than merely teaching people about portion control. Nevertheless, several of the scientific researched about this low-carb diet featured licensed dietitians assisting respondents in making food decisions, rather than the self-directed approach used by most people. This has been seen in other diet studies, according to the researchers, and the tests' results seem to be more positive in the real world than the weight loss.

Finally, a simple comparison between low-carb versus low-fat dieting revealed that there was a statistically significant difference in the amount of weight lost over a year. Low-carbohydrate dieters dropped an average of 13 pounds (6 kg), compared to 11.7 pounds for low-fat dieters (5.3 kg).

Ketogenic diets may help us lose weight, but they are no more successful than other diet methods. Since carbohydrate reserves in the body comprise water molecules, the bulk of the weight lost during the early stages of a ketogenic diet is water weight. This gives the scale an exciting amount at first, but weight reduction slows down with time.

What are the keto effects, and how can they help?

The advantages of a keto diet are close to that of other high-fat, low-carb diets, but it tends to be more successful than centrist low-carb diets. Keto is a low-carb, high-fat diet that maximizes health benefits. However, it will slightly raise the likelihood of complications.

Aid in weight loss

Weight reduction can be improved by converting the body into a fat-burning device. Insulin levels – the hormone that retains fat – are falling rapidly, suggesting that fat burning has risen dramatically. This seems to make it much easier to lose bodyweight without going hungry.

More than thirty high-quality observational studies show that low-carb and keto diets are more effective than other diets at losing weight.

Reverse type 2 diabetes by regulating blood sugar

A ketogenic diet has been shown in research to be successful in the treatment of type 2 diabetes, with total disease reversal occurring in certain instances. It makes perfect sense since keto removes the need for therapy, lowers blood sugar levels, and eliminates the potential negative consequences of high insulin levels.

Since a keto diet will reverse type 2 diabetes, it is likely to be helpful in preventing and reversing pre-diabetes. Keep in mind that "reversal" in this context refers to changing the disease, improving glucose tolerance, and reducing the need for care. It may be so drastically altered that after therapy, blood pressure returns to normal with time. In this context, reversal refers to progressing or deteriorating in the reverse direction of the condition. Changes in your lifestyle, on the other side, just succeed if you bring them into effect. If a person returns to the way of life he or she has before diabetes type 2 appeared and advanced, it is possible that success would return with time.

Improve your mental and physical performance:

Some people use ketogenic diets to boost their mental performance. It's also normal for people to feel more energized while they're in ketosis.

They don't need nutritional carbs for the brain on keto. It runs on ketones 24 hours a day, seven days a week, with a small amount of glucose synthesized in the liver. Carbohydrates are not necessary for the diet. As a result, ketosis leads to a steady flow of food (ketones) to the brain, avoiding significant blood sugar spikes. This will also assist with improved focus and attention, as well as clearing brain fog and improving mental awareness.

Epilepsy Treatment

The keto diet has been used to manage epilepsy since the 19th and 20th centuries and has proved to be effective. It has historically been used mainly for adolescents, although in recent years, it has also proved to be useful to adults. Or, used in conjunction with a keto diet, certain people with epilepsy might be able to take less to no anti-epileptic drugs while being seizure-free. This may help to reduce the drug's adverse effects while still improving cognitive capacity.

Keto Chaffle Recipes

1 Oreo Chaffles

(Ready in about 23 minutes | Serving 2 | Difficulty: Easy)

Per serving: Kcal 1381, Fat: 146g, Net Carbs: 14g, Protein: 17g

Ingredients

- 1/2 cup of Sugar-Free Chocolate Chips
- 1 tsp of Vanilla extract
- 3 Eggs
- 1/2 cup of butter
- 1/4 cup of sweetener

Cheese Frosting

- 4 ounces of Cream Cheese
- 4 ounces of butter
- 1/2 cup of Powdered Swerve
- 1 tsp of Vanilla extract
- 1/4 cup of Whipping Cream

Instructions

Melt chocolate and butter in a bowl in the microwave for around 1 minute. Stir to remove clumps. Mix vanilla, egg and sweetener in a bowl. Pour a quarter of the mixture into the waffle maker and cook for around 8 minutes. Mix frosting ingredients in the food processor's bowl in the meantime and make a smooth mixture. Spread frosting among two chaffles.

2 Strawberry Chaffles

(Ready in about 35 minutes | Serving 8 | Difficulty: Moderate)

Per serving: Kcal 189, Fat: 14.3g, Net Carbs: 5.2g, Protein: 10g

Ingredients

- 3 oz of cream cheese
- 1 cup of whipped cream
- 2 beaten eggs
- 2 cups shredded mozzarella cheese
- 1/2 cup of almond flour
- 2 tsp of baking powder
- 3 tbsp of sweetener
- 8 strawberries
- 1 tbsp of sweetener

Instructions

Add mozzarella and cream cheese to a bowl and microwave for around 1 minute. Beat eggs and mix with baking powder, 3 tbsp sweetener and almond flour. Mix it with cheese and add to 2 diced strawberries. Place in the fridge for around 20 minutes. Dice the rest of the strawberries and add tbsp sweetener. Warm waffle iron and add the quarter mixture from the fridge to the center of the iron. Cook for around 7 minutes.

©MidgetMomma.com

3 Chocolate Chaffle

(Ready in about 18 minutes | Serving 2 | Difficulty: Easy)

Per serving: Kcal 672, Fat: 70g, Net Carbs: 11g, Protein: 13g

Ingredients

- 1/2 cup of Chocolate Chips
- 1/4 cup of sweetener
- 3 Eggs
- 1/2 cup of butter
- 1 tsp of Vanilla extract

Instructions

Melt chocolate and butter in a bowl in the microwave for around 1 minute. Stir and remove clumps. Blend sweetener, vanilla and eggs in a bowl. Add chocolate and butter and whisk. Pour the quarter amount of mixture into a waffle maker. Cook for around 8 minutes.

4 Pumpkin Chaffles

(Ready in about 7 minutes | Serving 1 | Difficulty: Easy)

Per serving: Kcal 250, Fat: 15g, Net Carbs: 5g, Protein: 23g

Ingredients

- 1/2 cup mozzarella cheese shredded
- 1 1/2tbsp of pumpkin purée
- 1 beaten egg
- 1/2tsp of Swerve confectioners
- 1/4tsp of Pumpkin Pie Spice
- 1/2tsp of vanilla extract
- ⅛ tsp of maple extract

Instructions

Mix all the ingredients except mozzarella cheese in a bowl and mix. Add cheese and whisk. Spray waffle using cooking spray. Place half amount of batter in the center of the waffle maker. Cook for around 6 minutes. Repeat with the remaining batter.

5 Basic Chaffle

(Ready in about 8 minutes | Serving 2 | Difficulty: Easy)

Per serving: Kcal 208, Fat: 16g, Net Carbs: 4g, Protein: 11g

Ingredients

- 1 Big Egg
- 2 tbsp of Almond Flour
- 1/2 cup shredded Mozzarella cheese

Instructions

Preheat waffle iron for around 5 minutes. Microwave cheese for around 30 seconds. Add the rest of the ingredients and mix. Pour mixture that covers the surface of the waffle maker. Cook for around 4 minutes. Take out and place on a plate and repeat with the rest of the batter.

6 Garlic Chaffles

(Ready in about 8 minutes | Serving 2 | Difficulty: Easy)

Per serving: Kcal 208, Fat: 16g, Net Carbs: 4g, Protein: 11g

Ingredients

- 1/3 cup Parmesan cheese Grated
- 1/2 cup shredded Mozzarella cheese
- 1 Big Egg
- 1/2 tsp of Italian seasoning
- 1 minced Garlic clove

Instructions

Preheat waffle iron for around 5 minutes. Microwave cream cheese for around 30 seconds. Add the rest of the ingredients except the toppings. Pour mixture that covers the surface of the waffle maker. Cook for around 4 minutes. Take out and place on a plate and repeat with the rest of the batter.

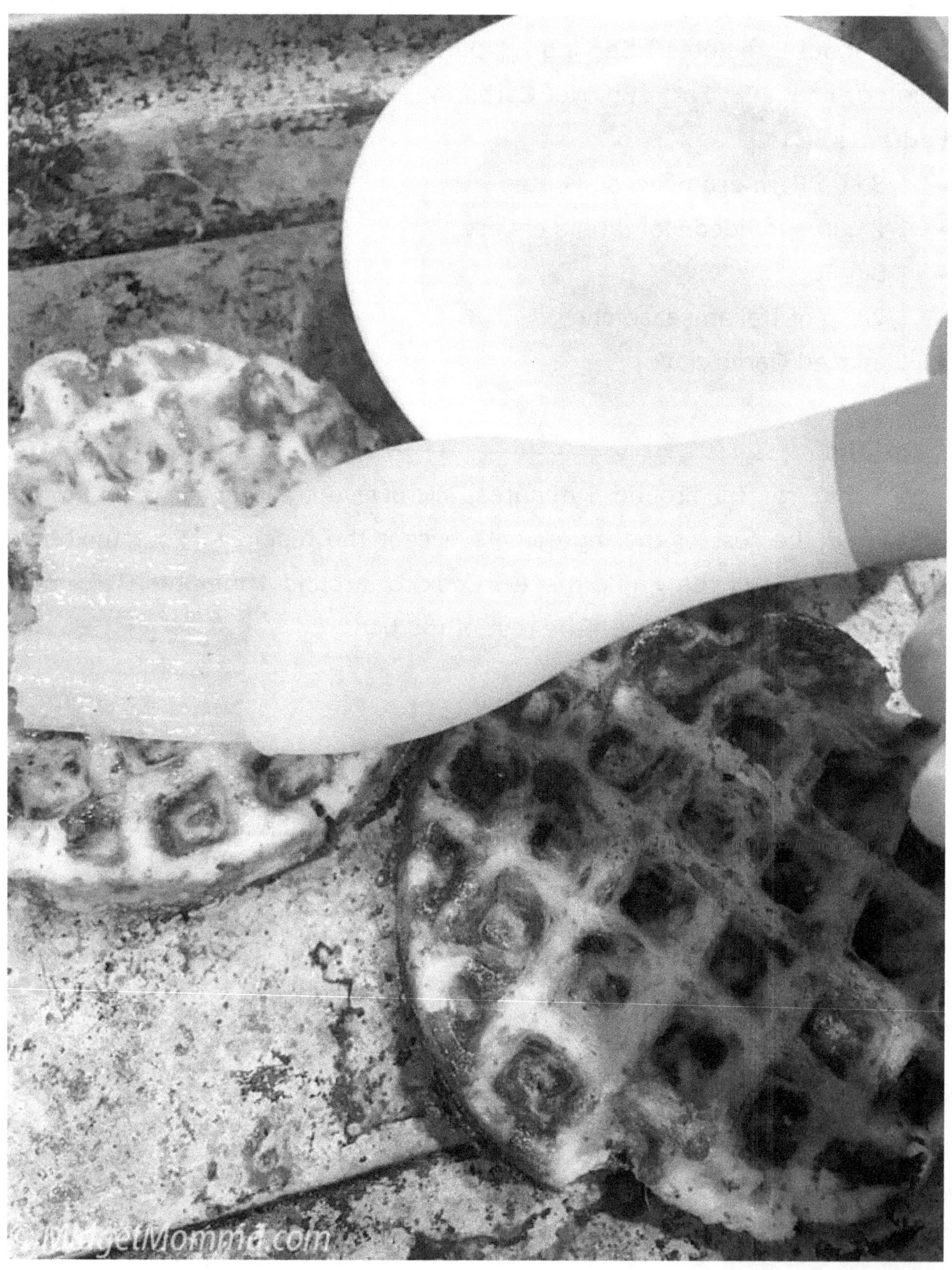

© MidgetMomma.com

7 Cinnamon Chaffles

(Ready in about 8 minutes | Serving 2 | Difficulty: Easy)

Per serving: Kcal 208, Fat: 16g, Net Carbs: 4g, Protein: 11g

Ingredients

- 3/4 cup shredded Mozzarella cheese
- 1 Big Egg
- 2 tbsp of Almond Flour
- 2 tbsp of besti erythritol
- 1/2 tbsp melted butter
- 1/2 tsp of cinnamon
- 1 tbsp melted butter
- 1/2 tsp of vanilla extract
- 3/4 tsp of cinnamon
- 1/4 cup of besti erythritol

Instructions

Preheat waffle iron for around 5 minutes. Microwave cream cheese for around 30 seconds. Add the rest of the ingredients except the toppings. Pour mixture that covers the surface of the waffle maker. Cook for around 4 minutes. Take out and place on a plate and repeat with the rest of the batter. To prepare churro chaffles, mix cinnamon and erythritol for topping. Brush chaffles using butter after they are cooked and sprinkle with topping.

8 Cheese Chaffles

(Ready in about 8 minutes | Serving 2 | Difficulty: Easy)

Per serving: Kcal 208, Fat: 16g, Net Carbs: 4g, Protein: 11g

Ingredients

- 1 Egg
- 1/2 oz of Cream cheese
- 1/2 cup shredded Mozzarella cheese
- 2 1/2 tbsp of Besti Erythritol
- 2 tbsp of pumpkin puree
- 1/2 tbsp of Pumpkin pie spice
- 3 tsp of Coconut Flour

Instructions

Preheat waffle iron for around 5 minutes. Microwave cream cheese for around 30 seconds. Add the rest of the ingredients except the toppings. Pour mixture that covers the surface of the waffle maker. Cook for around 4 minutes. Take out and place on a plate and repeat with the rest of the batter.

9 Spicy Chaffles

(Ready in about 8 minutes | Serving 2 | Difficulty: Easy)

Per serving: Kcal 208, Fat: 16g, Net Carbs: 4g, Protein: 11g

Ingredients

- 1 Egg
- 1 oz of Cream cheese
- 1 cup shredded Cheddar cheese
- 1/2 tbsp of Jalapenos
- 2 tbsp of Bacon bits

Instructions

Preheat waffle iron for around 5 minutes. Microwave cream cheese for around 30 seconds. Add the rest of the ingredients except the toppings. Pour mixture that covers the surface of the waffle maker. Cook for around 4 minutes. Take out and place on a plate and repeat with the rest of the batter.

10 Double Chocolate Chaffles

(Ready in about 5 minutes | Serving 1 | Difficulty: Easy)

Per serving: Kcal 197, Fat: 23.3g, Net Carbs: 11.3g, Protein: 24.3g

Ingredients

- 1 egg
- 1 tbsp of granulated sweetener
- 1/2 cup grated mozzarella
- 1 tsp of vanilla
- 1 tbsp of chocolate chips
- 2 tbsp of almond meal/flour
- 1 tsp of heavy cream
- 2 tbsp unsweetened cocoa powder

Instructions

Add all the ingredients to a bowl and mix. Preheat the waffle maker. Spray with oil and pour half amount of batter into the maker. Cook for around 4 minutes. Sprinkle with toppings and enjoy.

11 Vanilla Chaffles

(Ready in about 10 minutes | Serving 1 | Difficulty: Easy)

Per serving: Kcal 184, Fat: 20.1g, Net Carbs: 5.4g, Protein: 22.2g

Ingredients

- 1/2 cup of grated mozzarella
- 1 tbsp of granulated sweetener
- 1 eggs
- 1 tsp of vanilla extract
- 1 tbsp of chocolate chips
- 2 tbsp of almond flour

Instructions

Combine all the ingredients in a bowl. Preheat the waffle maker and spray it using oil once it is hot. Pour half amount of batter in the maker and cook for around 4 minutes. Remove and do the same with the rest of the batter. Top and enjoy.

12 Lemon Curd Chaffle

(Ready in about 50 minutes | Serving 3 | Difficulty: Hard)

Per serving: Kcal 302, Fat: 24g, Net Carbs: 6g, Protein: 15g

Ingredients

- 3 eggs
- one batch of lemon curd
- 4 ounces softened cream cheese
- 1 tsp of vanilla extract
- 1 tbsp sweetener low carb
- 3/4 cup shredded mozzarella cheese
- 1 tsp of baking powder
- 3 tbsp of coconut flour
- 1/3 tsp of salt

Instructions

Prepare lemon curd according to package instructions. Heat the maker and spray oil. Mix baking powder, salt and coconut flour in a bowl. Add the rest of the ingredients to another bowl and beat using a hand blender. Mix the two bowls mixture and pour in the maker. Cook for around 5 minutes. Top using lemon curd.

13 Glazed Donut

(Ready in about 15 minutes | Serving 3 | Difficulty: Easy)
Per serving: Kcal 246, Fat: 17g, Net Carbs: 2g, Protein: 14g

Ingredients

For chaffles

- 1/2 cup shredded cheese Mozzarella
- 2 tbsp of whey protein
- 1 ounce of Cream Cheese
- 2 tbsp of Swerve confectioners
- 1/2tsp of Vanilla extract
- 1/2tsp of Baking powder
- 1 Egg

For glaze

- 1/2tsp of Vanilla extract
- 3-4 tbsp of Swerve confectioners
- 2 tbsp of whipping cream

Instructions

Preheat the waffle maker. Add cream cheese and mozzarella in a bowl and microwave for around 30 seconds. Add 2 tbsp sweetener, whey protein and baking powder and mix. Add dough to a bowl and break an egg into it and add vanilla. Stir to form a smooth mixture. Add batter to the waffle maker and cook for around 5 minutes. Beat glaze ingredients in a bowl and top chaffles with it.

14 Nut-Free Chaffles

(Ready in about 30 minutes | Serving 3 | Difficulty: Easy)

Per serving: Kcal 195, Fat: 15.1g, Net Carbs: 31.5g, Protein: 8.5g

Ingredients

Batter

- 1/2 cup shredded cheese mozzarella
- 1/4 tsp of vanilla extract
- 2 tbsp of SunButter
- 2 tbsp of fruit sweetener
- 1 egg
- 2 tsp of cinnamon
- 1 tbsp of coconut flour
- ⅛ tsp of baking powder

Frosting

- 1 tbsp of cream cheese
- 1/4 cup of fruit sweetener
- 3/4 tbsp of butter, melted
- 1 tbsp of coconut milk unsweetened
- 1/4 tsp of vanilla extract

Coating

- 1 tsp of fruit sweetener
- 1 tsp of cinnamon

Instructions

Preheat the waffle iron. Mix batter ingredients in a bowl and place aside. Mix frosting ingredients except for coconut milk in a bowl and whisk until smooth. Add coconut milk and mix again. Place aside. Coat iron with cooking spray and add batter. Cook for around 4 minutes. Sprinkle with sweetener and cinnamon.

15 Chicken Chaffle

(Ready in about 19 minutes | Serving 2 | Difficulty: Easy)

Per serving: Kcal 675, Fat: 52g, Net Carbs: 8g, Protein: 44g

Ingredients

- 1/4 cup of almond flour
- 1/4 cup crumbled feta cheese
- 2 eggs
- 1 tsp of baking powder
- 1/2 cup shredded chicken
- 1/4 cup of Hot Sauce
- 1/4 cup shredded mozzarella cheese
- 3/4 cup shredded cheddar cheese
- 1/4 cup diced celery

Instructions

Mix almond flour and baking powder in a bowl. Preheat iron and spray using cooking spray. Beat eggs in a bowl and add hot sauce. Combine thoroughly and pour flour mixture. Combine and add grated cheeses. Fold in chicken. Pour in the maker and cook for around 4 minutes. Top with celery and feta.

16 Chaffle Sandwich

(Ready in about 13 minutes | Serving 1 | Difficulty: Easy)
Per serving: Kcal 238, Fat: 18g, Net Carbs: 2g, Protein: 17g

Ingredients
For chaffles

- 1/2 cup shredded Cheddar cheese
- 1 egg

For sandwich

- 1 tbsp of mayonnaise
- 2 slices of tomato
- 2 strips of bacon
- 3 pieces of lettuce

Instructions

Preheat the maker and mix cheese and egg in a bowl. Pour batter into the maker and cook for around 4 minutes. Do it in 2 batches. Cook bacon in pan paced on the moderate flame until it gets crispy. Drain using paper towels and form a sandwich using tomato, mayonnaise and lettuce.

17 Sausage Gravy Chaffle

(Ready in about 15 minutes | Serving 2 | Difficulty: Easy)

Per serving: Kcal 212, Fat: 17g, Net Carbs: 3g, Protein: 11g

Ingredients

For Chaffle

- 1/2 cup grated mozzarella cheese
- 1 egg
- 1 tsp of coconut flour
- 1/4 tsp of baking powder
- 1 tsp of water
- Salt

For Gravy

- 3 tbsp of chicken broth
- 1/4 cup browned breakfast sausage
- 2 tbsp of whipping cream
- dash of garlic powder
- 2 tsp softened cream cheese
- pepper

Instructions

Preheat the maker and coat using cooking spray. Add all ingredients to a bowl and mix. Pour half amount to mixture into the maker and cook for around 4 minutes. Repeat with the remaining batter and enjoy. Prepare breakfast sausage and add in the pan with remaining ingredients and boil. Reduce flame and cook for around 7 minutes to thicken it. Add pepper and salt and spoon gravy on top of chaffles.

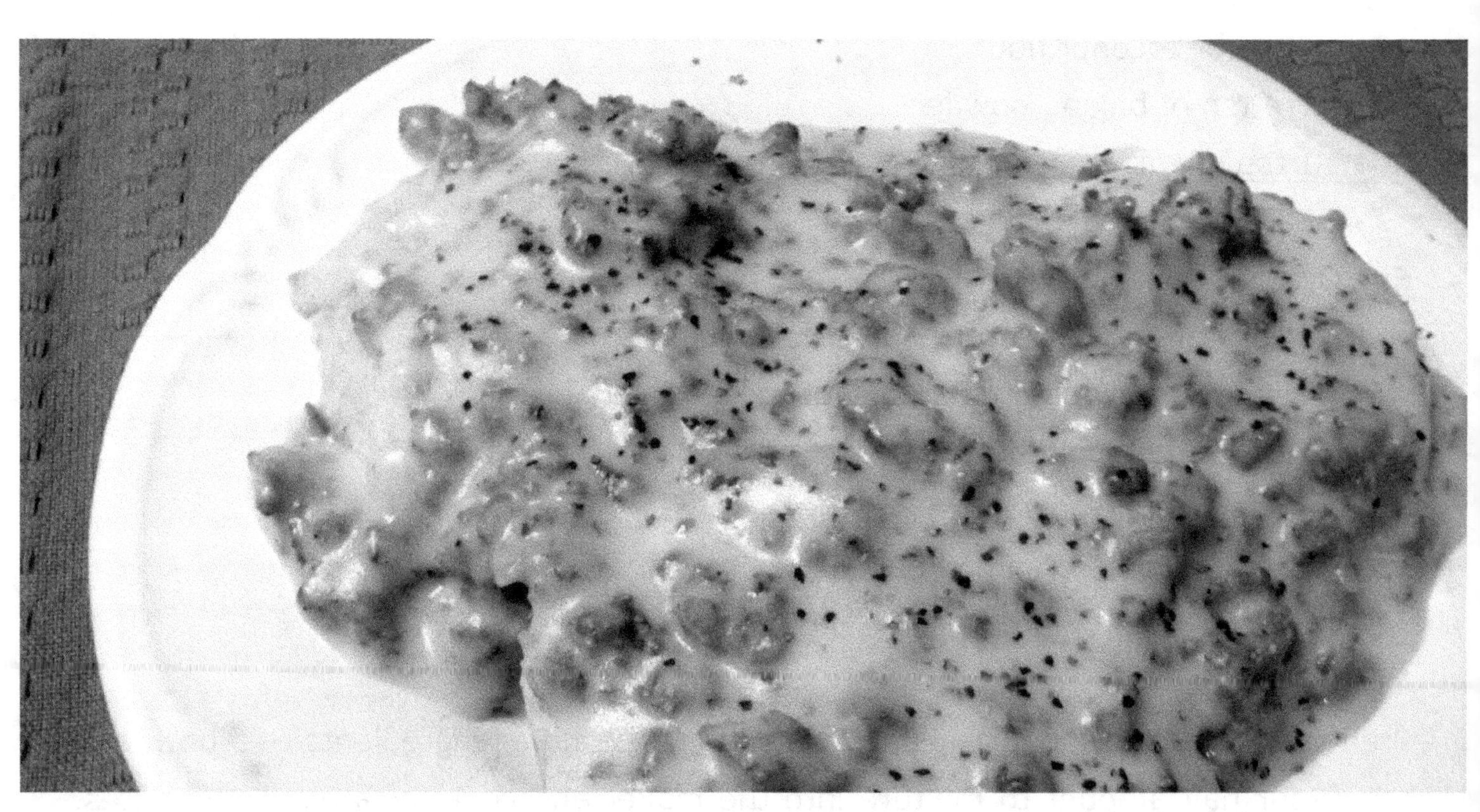

18 Eggs Benedict

(Ready in about 30 minutes | Serving 2 | Difficulty: Easy)
Per serving: Kcal 844, Fat: 78g, Net Carbs: 5g, Protein: 32g

Ingredients
For Chaffles
- 1/2 cup of mozzarella cheese
- 2 tbsp of almond flour
- 2 whites of eggs
- 1 tbsp of sour cream

For Hollandaise
- 2 tbsp of lemon juice
- 4 yolks of eggs
- 1/2 cup of salted butter

For Eggs
- 1 tbsp of white vinegar
- 3 ounces of deli ham
- 2 eggs

Instructions

Whisk eggs in a bowl and with the rest of the ingredients and blend. Preheat the waffle maker. Spray using cooking spray and add half the mixture. Cook for around 7 minutes. Make hollandaise sauce by forming a double broiler. Boil water and warm butter in the microwave. Add egg to bowl of the boiler. Boil and add hot butter while the pot is carried to a boil. Cook until egg thickens and take out of the bowl. Drizzle lemon juice and place aside. Warm chaffle using toaster and top with ham slices, 2 tbsp hollandaise sauce and one egg.

19 Garlic Chaffle

(Ready in about 10 minutes | Serving 8 | Difficulty: Easy)

Per serving: Kcal 74, Fat: 6.5g, Net Carbs: 0.9g, Protein: 3.4g

Ingredients

- 1 egg
- 2 tbsp of almond flour
- 1/2 cup grated mozzarella cheese
- 1/2tsp of garlic powder
- 1/2tsp of salt
- 1/2tsp of oregano

Topping

- 1/2tsp of garlic powder
- 2 tbsp softened butter
- 1/4 cup grated mozzarella cheese

Instructions

Preheat the maker and oil it. Mix ingredients except topping ingredients. Pour into the maker and cook for around 5 minutes. Mix garlic powder and butter and pour over waffle. Sprinkle with mozzarella and cook for around 3 minutes.

© MidgetMomma.com

20 Taco Chaffle

(Ready in about 13 minutes | Serving 1 | Difficulty: Easy)

Per serving: Kcal 258, Fat: 19g, Net Carbs: 4g, Protein: 18g

Ingredients

- 1/4 cup shredded jack cheese
- 1 white of egg
- 1/4 cup shredded cheddar cheese
- 1 tsp of coconut flour
- 3/4 tsp of water
- 1/4 tsp of baking powder
- pinch of salt
- 1/8 tsp of chili powder

Instructions

Preheat the maker and oil it. Combine everything in a bowl and spoon half amount of mixture in the maker. Cook for around 4 minutes. Remove the chaffle shell and place it aside. Repeat with the remaining batter. Turn the pan and position shells of the chaffle among cups to make a shell of taco.

© LowCarbInspirations.com

21 Pizza Chaffle

(Ready in about 8 minutes | Serving 2 | Difficulty: Easy)

Per serving: Kcal 76, Fat: 4.3g, Net Carbs: 4.1g, Protein: 5.5g

Ingredients

- 1 egg
- Pinch of Italian seasoning
- 1/2 cup shredded mozzarella cheese
- 1 tbsp of pizza sauce

Instructions

Preheat the maker. Whisk eggs in a bowl and add seasonings. Mix shredded cheese in a bowl. Add half amount of mixture to the maker and cook for around 4 minutes. Repeat with the rest of the batter and with 1 tbsp pizza sauce and pepperoni.

22 Parmesan Chaffles

(Ready in about 6 minutes | Serving 1 | Difficulty: Easy)

Per serving: Kcal 352, Fat: 24g, Net Carbs: 2g, Protein: 14g

Ingredients

- 1 beaten egg
- 1/2 cup of mozzarella cheese shredded
- 1/4 cup of Parmesan cheese grated
- 1/4tsp of garlic powder
- 1 tsp of Italian seasoning

Instructions

Preheat the waffle maker. Add all the ingredients except mozzarella and parmesan cheese in a bowl and mix. Mix the cheese in a bowl and spray waffle sung cooking spray. Pour half amount of mixture in the maker and cook for around 5 minutes. Top using parmesan and enjoy.

CHICKEN PARMESAN
Chaffle

23 Italian Chaffle

(Ready in about 6 minutes | Serving 1 | Difficulty: Easy)

Per serving: Kcal 352, Fat: 24g, Net Carbs: 2g, Protein: 14g

Ingredients

- 1 beaten egg
- 1/2 cup of mozzarella cheese shredded
- 1/4 cup of Parmesan cheese grated
- 1/4tsp of garlic powder
- 1 tsp of Italian seasoning

Instructions

Preheat the waffle maker. Add all the ingredients except mozzarella and parmesan cheese in a bowl and mix. Mix the cheese in a bowl and spray waffle sung cooking spray. Pour half amount of mixture in the maker and cook for around 5 minutes. Top using parmesan and add lettuce, cold cuts, tomato.

24 Chaffle Breadsticks

(Ready in about 6 minutes | Serving 1 | Difficulty: Easy)

Per serving: Kcal 352, Fat: 24g, Net Carbs: 2g, Protein: 14g

Ingredients

- 1 beaten egg
- 1/2 cup of mozzarella cheese shredded
- Marinara sauce
- 1/4 cup of Parmesan cheese grated
- 1/4tsp of garlic powder
- 1 tsp of Italian seasoning

Instructions

Preheat the waffle maker. Add all the ingredients except mozzarella and parmesan cheese in a bowl and mix. Mix the cheese in a bowl and spray waffle sung cooking spray. Pour half amount of mixture in the maker and cook for around 5 minutes. Top using parmesan and dice into 4 sticks and enjoy with Marinara Sauce.

25 Chaffle Bruschetta

(Ready in about 6 minutes | Serving 1 | Difficulty: Easy)

Per serving: Kcal 352, Fat: 24g, Net Carbs: 2g, Protein: 14g

Ingredients

- 1 beaten egg
- 1/2 cup of mozzarella cheese shredded
- 1/4 cup of Parmesan cheese grated
- Basil
- Olive oil
- 1/4tsp of garlic powder
- 1 tsp of Italian seasoning

Instructions

Preheat the waffle maker. Add all the ingredients except mozzarella and parmesan cheese in a bowl and mix. Mix the cheese in a bowl and spray waffle sung cooking spray. Pour half amount of mixture in the maker and cook for around 5 minutes. Top using parmesan and mix 4 chopped cherry tomatoes, ½ tsp chopped fresh basil, drop of olive oil and salt. Add on chaffle.

26 Cauliflower Chaffles

(Ready in about 9 minutes | Serving 2 | Difficulty: Easy)

Per serving: Kcal 246, Fat: 16g, Net Carbs: 7g, Protein: 20g

Ingredients

- 1/4 tsp of Garlic Powder
- 1 cup of riced cauliflower
- 1/4 tsp of Ground Black Pepper
- 1/4 tsp of Kosher Salt
- 1/2 tsp of Italian seasoning
- 1 Eggs
- 1/2 cup of mozzarella cheese shredded
- 1/2 cup of parmesan cheese shredded

Instructions

Blend all ingredients except the cauliflower mixture and parmesan cheese in a blender and sprinkle half parmesan in the maker. Pour mixture in maker and top with cauliflower mixture and rest of parmesan. Cook for around 5 minutes.

27 Zucchini Chaffles

(Ready in about 15 minutes | Serving 2 | Difficulty: Easy)

Per serving: Kcal 194, Fat: 13g, Net Carbs: 4g, Protein: 16g

Ingredients

- 1 beaten Egg
- 1/2 tsp Black Pepper Ground
- 1 cup grated Zucchini
- 1/2 cup of parmesan cheese shredded
- 1 tsp chopped Dried Basil
- 1/4 cup of mozzarella cheese shredded
- 3/4 tsp divided Kosher Salt

Instructions

Sprinkle 1/4 tsp salt on zucchini. Beat egg in a bowl and add mozzarella, zucchini, 1/2 tsp salt, basil and pepper. Sprinkle 2 tbsp parmesan on iron and spread a quarter of zucchini mixture on the maker. Top using 2 tbsp parmesan and cook for around 8 minutes. Repeat with the rest of the mixture.

28 Peanut Chaffles

(Ready in about 6 minutes | Serving 2 | Difficulty: Easy)

Per serving: Kcal 264, Fat: 21.6g, Net Carbs: 7.25g, Protein: 9.45g

Ingredients

Chaffle

- 1 Egg
- 1/4 tsp of Baking Powder
- 1 tbsp of Unsweetened Cocoa
- 1 tbsp of Heavy Cream
- 1 tbsp of Powdered Sweetener
- 1/2 tsp of Vanilla Extract
- 1 tsp of Coconut Flour
- 1/2 tsp of Batter Flavor

Butter Filling

- 2 tsp of Powdered Sweetener
- 3 tbsp of Peanut Butter
- 2 tbsp of Heavy Cream

InstructionsPreheat the maker. Combine ingredients of chaffle in a bowl and pour half amount of mixture in maker. Cook for around 5 minutes. Repeat with the rest of the mixture. Blend butter ingredients and spread over chaffles.

29 Easy Chaffle Recipe

(Ready in about 10 minutes | Serving 2| Difficulty: Easy)

Ingredients
Simple Chaffles

Per serving: Kcal 152, Fat: 8g, Net Carbs: 1g, Protein: 9g

- 1 Egg
- 1/2 Cup of Shredded Cheese Mozarella

Instructions

Add all ingredients to a bowl and whisk to combine. Coat waffle maker using cooking spray and pour half amount of batter into the maker. Cook for around 5 minutes and repeat with the rest of the batter.

30 Savory Chaffles

Per serving: Kcal 215, Fat: 16.5g, Net Carbs: 2g, Protein: 12g

- 1 Egg
- 1/2 Cup Shredded Cheese Mozarella
- 1/16 Tsp of Xanthan Gum
- 1/4 Cup of Almond Flour

Instructions

Add all ingredients to a bowl and whisk to combine. Coat waffle maker using cooking spray and pour half amount of batter into the maker. Cook for around 5 minutes and repeat with the rest of the batter.

31 Sweet Chaffles

Per serving: Kcal 192, Fat: 15gg, Net Carbs: 1.55g, Protein: 15g

- 1 Egg
- 1/2 Cup of Shredded Cheese Mozzarella
- 1/4 Cup of Almond Flour
- 1/16 Tsp of Xanthan Gum
- 2 Tbsp of Confectioners Swerve

Instructions

Add all ingredients to a bowl and whisk to combine. Coat waffle maker using cooking spray and pour half amount of batter into the maker. Cook for around 5 minutes and repeat with the rest of the batter.

32 Tasty Chaffles

(Ready in about 13 minutes | Serving 2 | Difficulty: Easy)

Per serving: Kcal 116, Fat: 9.5gg, Net Carbs: 2.6g, Protein: 4.5g

Ingredients

- 1 oz softened cream cheese
- 1 tbsp of almond flour
- 1 tbsp of pumpkin puree
- 1 egg
- 1/2 tsp of pumpkin spice

Instructions

Whisk the cream cheese in a bowl. Whisk pumpkin puree and egg in a bowl. Add almond flour and pumpkin spice and mix. Preheat the iron and spray using oil. Pour half amount of mixture in the maker and cook for around 5 minutes. Repeat with the rest of the batter.

© MidgetMomma.com

33 Bread Sticks Chaffle

(Ready in about 12 minutes | Serving 7 | Difficulty: Easy)

Per serving: Kcal 80, Fat: 7g, Net Carbs: 1g, Protein: 5g

Ingredients

- 1 egg
- 2 tbsp of almond flour
- 1/2 cup grated mozzarella cheese
- 1/2tsp of garlic powder
- 1/2tsp of salt
- 1/2tsp of oregano

Topping

- 1/2tsp of garlic powder
- 2 tbsp softened butter
- 1/4 cup grated mozzarella cheese

Instructions

Preheat the maker and oil it. Mix all ingredients except topping ingredients. Pour in the maker and cook for around 5 minutes. Make four strips of waffle. Mix butter and garlic powder and coat strips with it. Sprinkle with mozzarella and cook for around 3 minutes.

34 Original Chaffle

(Ready in about 5 minutes | Serving 1 | Difficulty: Easy)

Per serving: Kcal 246, Fat: 18g, Net Carbs: 2g, Protein: 17g

Ingredients

- 2 eggs
- 1/4 cup of almond flour
- 1/2 cup of mozzarella
- 1/2 tsp of baking powder

Instructions

Preheat iron and spray with cooking spray. Mix all the ingredients in a bowl and pour half amount of the mixture into the maker. Cook for around 5 minutes and repeat with the rest of the mixture.

35 Mini Chaffles

(Ready in about 11 minutes | Serving 2 | Difficulty: Easy)
Per serving: Kcal 73, Fat: 6g, Net Carbs: 4g, Protein: 2g

Ingredients

- 2 tsp of Coconut Flour
- 1/4 tsp of Baking Powder
- 4 tsp of Swerve
- 1 Egg
- 1/2 tsp of Vanilla Extract
- 1 oz of Cream Cheese

Instructions

Preheat the iron. Add baking powder, coconut flour and swerve in a bowl and mix. Add cream cheese, egg and vanilla extract in bowl and mix. Pour mixture in the maker and cook for around 4 minutes.

36 Grain-free chaffles

(Ready in about 20 minutes | Serving 2 | Difficulty: Easy)

Per serving: Kcal 277, Fat: 20g, Net Carbs: 4.6g, Protein: 4.8g

Ingredients

- 1 tbsp of almond flour
- 1 tsp of vanilla
- 1 egg
- 1 shake of cinnamon
- 1 cup of mozzarella cheese
- 1 tsp of baking powder
- Butter

Instructions

Mix vanilla extract and egg in a bowl. Mix almond flour, baking powder and cinnamon. Add mozzarella cheese at the end and coat with the mixture evenly. Spray waffle using oil and turn it on. Pour mixture and cook for around 5 minutes. Top with butter and enjoy.

37 Healthy Chaffles

(Ready in about 20 minutes | Serving 4 | Difficulty: Easy)

Per serving: Kcal 411, Fat: 35g, Net Carbs: 6g, Protein: 21g

Ingredients

- 1 1/2 cup of shredded cheese cheddar
- 4 oz. cream cheese
- 4 eggs
- 2 tsp of baking powder
- 1/2 cup of almond flour
- Syrup

Instructions

Oil the waffle maker and mix all ingredients in a bowl. Pour batter into the maker and cook for around 5 minutes. Top with syrup(sugar-free) and enjoy.

38 Sunny Chaffle

(Ready in about 10 minutes | Serving 1 | Difficulty: Easy)

Per serving: Kcal 320, Fat: 24.3g, Net Carbs: 3.1g, Protein: 21.7g

Ingredients

- 1 egg
- Strawberries
- 2 tbsp of almond flour
- 1/2 cup of mozzarella cheese
- 1/2tsp of baking powder

Instructions

Preheat the maker and mix all the ingredients in a bowl. Pour into the center of the maker and cook for around 5 minutes. Top with strawberries and enjoy.

39 Traditional Chaffles

(Ready in about 13 minutes | Serving 1 | Difficulty: Easy)

Per serving: Kcal 291, Fat: 23g, Net Carbs: 1g, Protein: 20g

Ingredients

- 1/2 cup of shredded cheese cheddar
- 1 egg

Instructions

Preheat the maker and oil it gently. Break the egg in a bowl and add the half cup of cheddar cheese. Mix and pour half amount of mixture in maker. Cook for around 4 minutes. Repeat with the rest of the mixture.

40 Best Pizza Chaffle

(Ready in about 20 minutes | Serving 2 | Difficulty: Easy)

Per serving: Kcal 241, Fat: 18g, Net Carbs: 4g, Protein: 17g

Ingredients

- 1 tsp of coconut flour
- 1/2 cup of shredded cheese mozzarella
- 1 white of egg
- `1 tsp softened cream cheese
- 1/8 tsp of Italian seasoning
- 1/4 tsp of baking powder
- 1/8 tsp of garlic powder
- 3 tsp of marinara sauce
- Salt
- 1/2 cup of mozzarella cheese
- 1 tbsp shredded cheese parmesan
- 6 pepperonis diced in half
- 1/4 tsp of basil seasoning

Instructions

Preheat the oven to 400 degrees F. Preheat the maker as well. Add all the ingredients except pepperoni and parmesan cheese in a bowl and mix. Pour half amount of mixture in the maker and cook for around 4 minutes. Repeat with the rest of the mixture. Top with pepperoni, tomato sauce and parmesan cheese. Bake in the oven by placing on the top shelf for around 6 minutes. Turn broil setting and cook for around 2 minutes. Sprinkle with basil.

41 Open-Faced Chaffle

(Ready in about 17 minutes | Serving 2 | Difficulty: Easy)

Per serving: Kcal 118, Fat: 8g, Net Carbs: 2g, Protein: 9g

Ingredients

- 1 egg only white
- 1/4 cup shredded cheddar cheese
- 1/4 cup shredded cheese mozzarella
- 3/4 tsp of water
- 1/4 tsp of baking powder
- 1 tsp of coconut flour
- Salt

Instructions

Preheat the oven to 425 degrees F. Preheat the maker as well. Mix everything in a bowl and pour half the amount of mixture into a maker. Cook for around 4 minutes and repeat with the remaining mixture. Line parchment paper on a cookie sheet and place chaffles on it. Add a quarter cup of roasted keto beef gravy. Add cheese slice on top and bake in the oven for around 5 minutes in the top rack. Broil for around 1 minute.

42 Cream Chaffles

(Ready in about 15 minutes | Serving 2 | Difficulty: Easy)

Per serving: Kcal 293, Fat: 27g, Net Carbs: 5g, Protein: 10g

Ingredients

- 4 eggs
- 1 tsp of vanilla extract
- 2 tbsp of melted butter
- 4 oz of cream cheese
- 1 tsp of baking powder

Instructions

Blend all ingredients in a blender for around 1 minute. Spray the waffle maker using cooking spray and pour the mixture into the maker. Cook until it turns crispy and golden.

43 Fluffy Chaffles

(Ready in about 45 minutes | Serving 8 | Difficulty: Moderate)

Per serving: Kcal 140, Fat: 11g, Net Carbs: 4g, Protein: 4g

Ingredients

- 64 g of almond flour
- 1 1/2 tsp of baking powder
- 1 tbsp of ground psyllium husk
- 28 g of coconut flour
- 1 tsp of xanthan gum
- 57 g of butter
- 240 ml of water
- 3 tbsp of erythritol
- 3 eggs beaten
- 1/4 tsp of kosher salt
- 1 tsp of vanilla extract

Instructions

Mix flours, xantham gum and husk in a bowl. Warm water, sweetener, salt and butter in a pot and once it starts simmering, add flours and incorporate. Cook for around 3 minutes. Transfer dough to bowl and add egg one by one, mixing using an electric mixer. Add baking powder and vanilla extract and mix. Heat the maker and oil it. Pour batter and cook for around 12 minutes.

44 Almond Flour Chaffles

(Ready in about 20 minutes | Serving 2 | Difficulty: Easy)

Per serving: Kcal 70, Fat: 3.8g, Net Carbs: 4.9g, Protein: 4g

Ingredients

- 4 separated eggs
- 1/4 cup of granulated Swerve
- 2 cup of almond flour
- 2 tsp of baking powder
- 1/2 cup of butter
- 1 tsp of kosher salt
- 1/2 cup of almond butter
- Cooking spray
- 2 tsp. of vanilla extract
- Maple syrup

Instructions

Preheat waffle maker to high. Mix stevia, almond flour, salt and baking powder in a bowl. Melt almond butter and butter in the microwave for around 15 seconds. Stir dry ingredients with butter mixture and then add vanilla and yolks. Beat whites in a separate bowl and fold in batter. Spray maker using cooking spray and pour the batter. Cook for around 5 minutes. Top with maple syrup and butter.

©MidgetMom

45 Butter Chaffles

(Ready in about 30 minutes | Serving 5 | Difficulty: Easy)

Per serving: Kcal 216, Fat: 19.9g, Net Carbs: 5.5g, Protein: 6.4g

Ingredients

- 5 eggs
- 4 tbsp of granulated sweetener
- 4 tbsp of coconut flour
- 1 tsp of baking powder
- 3 tbsp of milk full fat
- 2 tsp of vanilla
- 125 g of butter melted

Instructions

Beat egg whites in a bowl. Mix yolks with sweetener, baking powder and coconut flour in a separate bowl. Add butter and mix. Add vanilla and milk and mix. Fold whites in yolk mixture and pour in maker. Cook for around 5 minutes.

46 Paleo Chaffles

(Ready in about 10minutes | Serving 2 | Difficulty: Easy)

Per serving: Kcal 401, Fat: 37, Net Carbs: 9g, Protein: 13g

Ingredients

- 1 egg
- 2 tbsp of sweetener
- 1/2 cup of Almond Flour
- 1/2 tsp of baking powder Gluten-free
- 2 tbsp of Almond butter
- 1/4 tsp of Sea salt
- 2 tbsp of Butter
- 1/2 tsp of Vanilla extract
- 1/4 cup of almond milk Unsweetened

Instructions

Preheat waffle maker to high temperature. Oil it gently and beat whites in a bowl. Combine baking powder, erythritol, salt and almond flour in another bowl. Melt almond butter and butter in the microwave and add to the flour mixture. Add yolk, vanilla and almond milk and stir. Fold whites in batter and mix. Pour in the maker and cook for around 5 minutes.

47 Crispy Chaffles

(Ready in about 10 minutes | Serving 4 | Difficulty: Easy)

Per serving: Kcal 64, Fat: 2g, Net Carbs: 4g, Protein: 5g

Ingredients

- 4 tbsp sifted coconut flour
- 1/4 tsp of baking powder
- 1 tsp of coconut oil
- 1 tbsp sweetener granulated
- 2/3 cup of egg whites
- 1/2 tsp of vanilla extract
- 1/4 cup of milk
- 1 tbsp of unsweetened apple sauce

Instructions

Mix sweetener, baking powder and coconut flour in a bowl. Add whites, vanilla, apple sauce and milk in a separate bowl and mix. Pour to the other bowl and form a thick batter. Add oil and spray waffle maker using cooking spray. Once the maker is hot, pour the batter and cook for around 4 minutes.

48 Salted Chaffles

(Ready in about 15 minutes | Serving 2 | Difficulty: Easy)

Per serving: Kcal 425, Fat: 36.7g, Net Carbs: 10.7g, Protein: 14.8g

Ingredients

Dry

- 3/4 cup of Almond Flour
- 1 tbsp of Coconut flour
- 2 tbsp of Erythritol
- 1 tsp of Baking Powder
- 1/8 tsp of Himalayan Salt

Wet

- 2 tbsp of Melted Butter
- 2 Eggs
- 2 tbsp of Cream Cheese at room temperature
- 1 tsp of Vanilla Extract

Instructions

Preheat waffle maker to high. Mix wet ingredients in a bowl. Mix dry ingredients in a separate bowl. Mix both bowls and pour in the maker. Cook for around 4 minutes.

©MidgetMomma.com

49 Low Carb Chaffles

(Ready in about 8 minutes | Serving 1 | Difficulty: Easy)

Per serving: Kcal 522, Fat: 48g, Net Carbs: 7g, Protein: 19g

Ingredients

- 2 eggs
- 1/2 tsp of baking powder
- 4 tbsp of almond flour
- 2 oz of cream cheese
- 1 tbsp of coconut oil

Instructions

Blend everything in the blender and pour in the maker, which is oiled. Cook for around 3 minutes.

50 Sweet Chaffles

(Ready in about 9 minutes | Serving 2 | Difficulty: Easy)
Per serving: Kcal 331, Fat: 29g, Net Carbs: 7g, Protein: 11g

Ingredients
Dry

- 1/2 cup of almond flour
- 1/2 tsp of sweetener
- 1/4tsp of baking soda
- 1/4tsp of salt
- 1/4 tsp of baking powder
- 1/8 tsp of nutmeg
- 1/4tsp of ground cinnamon
- 1/8 tsp of cloves

Wet

- 2 eggs
- 2 tbsp of melted butter
- 1 tsp of vanilla extract

Instructions

Add dry ingredients to a bowl and mix. Separate yolks and whites in two bowls and mix butter and vanilla in yolks. Beat whites and add yolks to dry ingredients. Then add whites while mixing gently. Preheat maker to high temperature and pour the mixture. Cook for around 5 minutes.

51 Churro Chaffle

(Ready in about 15 minutes | Serving 1 | Difficulty: Easy)

Per serving: Kcal 193, Fat: 14g, Net Carbs: 2g, Protein: 8g

Ingredients

- 1 egg
- 1/4 cup of almond flour
- 1 tsp of cinnamon
- 1/2 cup of shredded cheese mozzarella
- 2 tbsp of Swerve granular
- 2 tbsp of melted butter
- ⅛ tsp of baking powder
- 3 tbsp of Swerve granular

Instructions

Combine everything in a bowl and pour the mixture into the maker by dividing it into three parts. Melt butter in the meantime in a pan over moderate flame. Add churro toppings and enjoy.

© LowCarbInspirations.com

52 Avocado Egg Bake

(Ready in about 20 minutes | Serving 1 | Difficulty: Easy)

Per serving: Kcal 605, Fat: 50.9g, Net Carbs: 18.6g, Protein: 25.3g

Ingredients

- 2 eggs
- 1 avocado, pitted and halved
- ¼ cup of shredded Cheddar cheese
- 1 tbsp. chopped fresh parsley, or according to taste
- Freshly ground black pepper and salt according to taste

Instructions

- Preheat oven to 425 degrees Fahrenheit.
- To make way for one egg, scoop out some of the avocados from where the pit. Put each avocado half on the baking sheet, then crack one egg on top.
- Cook for fifteen to twenty minutes in a preheated oven before the egg is ready. Season with pepper and salt and finish with Cheddar cheese. Serve with new parsley as a garnish.

53 Oven-Baked Bacon

(Ready in about 35 minutes | Serving 6 | Difficulty: Easy)

Per serving: Kcal 134, Fat: 10.4g, Net Carbs: 0.4g, Protein: 9.2g

Ingredients

1 (16 oz.) package bacon

Instructions

- Preheat oven to 350°F. Using parchment paper, line a baking dish.
- Put the bacon slices on a prepared baking sheet, one on top of the other.
- Bake for fifteen to twenty minutes in a preheated oven. Take off the dish from the oven. Return the bacon slices to the oven after tossing them with kitchen tongs. Bake for another fifteen to twenty minutes, or till crispy. Thinner slices may require less time to cook, about twenty minutes overall. Drain on a paper towel-lined pan.

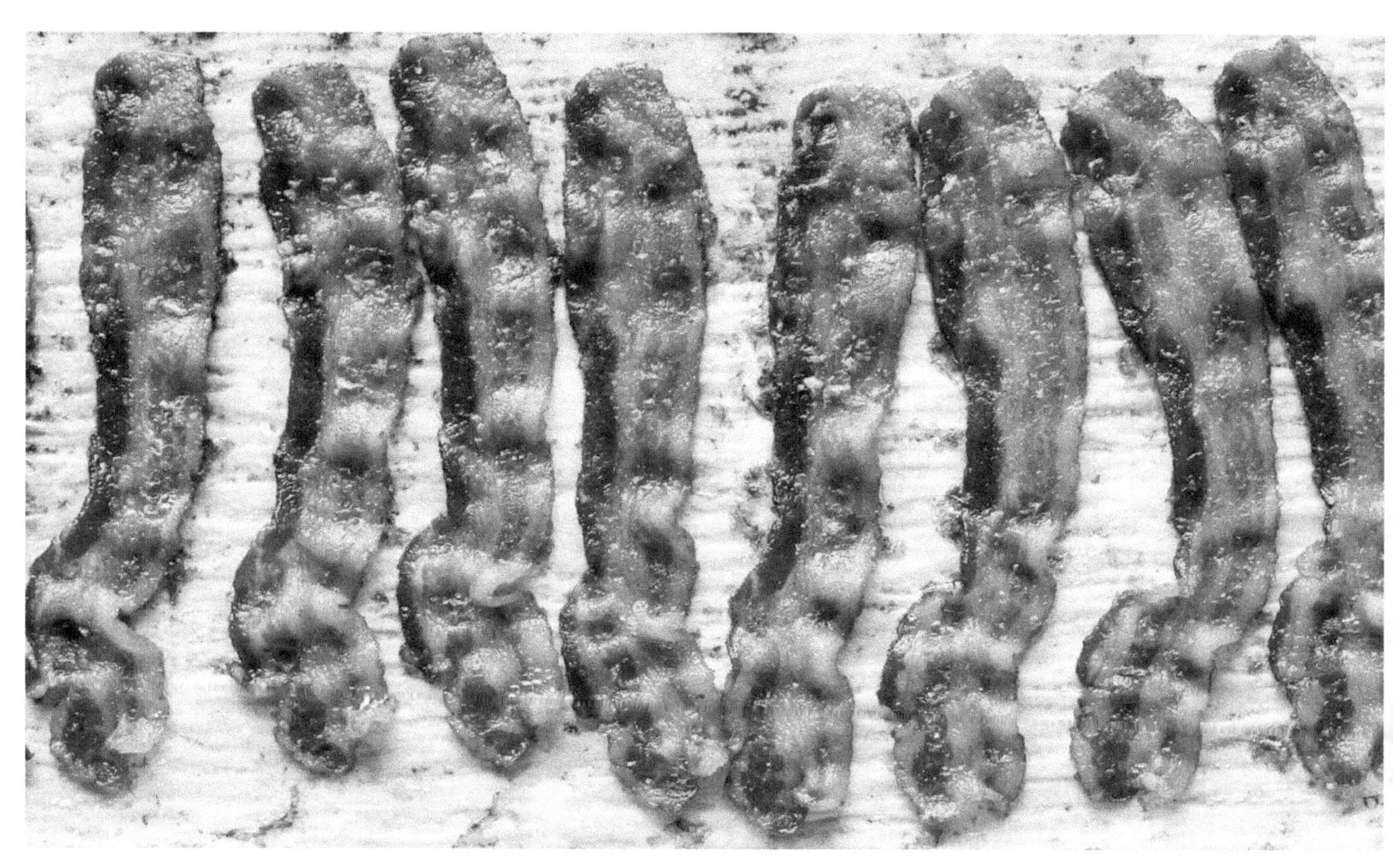

54 Roasted Leeks With Eggs

(Ready in about 40 minutes | Serving 2 | Difficulty: Easy)

Per serving: Kcal 1219, Fat: 124.6g, Net Carbs: 27.8g, Protein: 11.8g

Ingredients

- 3 green onions
- 2 leeks
- 2 tbsp. melted ghee (clarified butter)
- ¼ tsp. ground black pepper
- ½ tsp. sea salt

Avocado Vinaigrette:

- ¾ cup of light olive oil
- ⅛ tsp. red pepper flakes
- 1 ripe avocado, flesh scooped from the skin, pitted
- 1 lemon, juiced
- Ground black pepper and salt according to taste
- ¼ cup of red wine vinegar
- 1 tsp. olive oil
- ¼ cup of sliced, toasted almonds
- 2 eggs

Instructions

- Preheat oven to 400 degrees Fahrenheit.
- Green tops and bottom half-inch of the leeks should be discarded. Leeks can be sliced in half lengthwise.
- On a sheet tray, arrange the green onions and leeks. Drizzle ghee on top. Season with salt and pepper.
- For fifteen to twenty minutes in a preheated oven, roast till brown.
- In a food processor, thoroughly 3/4 cup olive oil, mix avocado, vinegar, lemon juice, pepper, and salt to make the vinaigrette

- In a skillet on medium-low flame, heat 1 tsp. oil for two to three minutes, or before whites are just set and the yolks are already runny, break eggs onto the opposite sides of the skillet.
- Remove the leeks and onions from the oven and put them on top with the sunny-side-up eggs. On top, sprinkle red pepper flakes and almonds. Finish with an avocado vinaigrette drizzle.

55 Gluten-Free Bagels

(Ready in about 30 minutes | Serving 6 | Difficulty: Easy)

Per serving: Kcal 364, Fat: 27.9g, Net Carbs: 9.7g, Protein: 20.9g

Ingredients

- 1 tbsp. baking powder, gluten-free
- 1 ½ cups of almond flour
- 2 eggs
- 1 tsp. garlic salt
- 2 oz. cream cheese, cubed
- 2 ½ cups of shredded mozzarella cheese

Instructions

- Preheat oven to 400 degrees Fahrenheit. Using parchment paper, line the baking sheet.
- In a mixing bowl, add the baking powder, garlic salt, and almond flour.
- In the microwave-safe bowl, mix mozzarella and cream cheese. Microwave for one minute, then remove and mix. Microwave for another minute, then take it off and stir until all is well combined. Working fast, stir the eggs and flour mixture into melted cheese mixture. Knead the dough by hand until It becomes a sticky dough. Continue kneading and pressing the dough for approximately two minutes or until it is fully uniform.
- The dough can be divided into six equal bits. Roll each one into the long log, then push the ends together to form a bagel shape and put it on the baking sheet that has been prepared.
- For ten to fourteen minutes in the preheated oven, bake till the bagels are golden.

55 Keto Zucchini Hash

(Ready in about 30 minutes | Serving 4 | Difficulty: Easy)

Per serving: Kcal 200, Fat: 17.9g, Net Carbs: 5g, Protein: g

Ingredients

- 3 tbsp. coconut oil
- 4 small zucchini, squeezed dry and grated
- 1 tbsp. butter
- 1 tsp. chili powder, or according to taste
- ⅓ cup of grated Parmesan cheese
- 1 tsp. sea salt
- 2 eggs, beaten
- 1 tsp. cayenne pepper (Optional)

Directions

- In a small skillet over medium flame, combine the coconut oil, butter, and zucchini. Add the chili powder, Parmesan cheese, cayenne pepper, and salt to a mixing bowl. Stir until the cheese has melted.
- Reduce the heat to a minimum and whisk in the eggs before thoroughly combined. Adjust to medium heat and fry, stirring and tossing sometimes, for almost fifteen minutes, or till the edges of hash are lightly browned.

Conclusion

A keto diet may be a healthier option for certain people, although the amount of fat, carbohydrates, and protein prescribed varies from person to person. If you have diabetes, talk to the doctor before starting the diet because it would almost certainly need prescription changes and stronger blood sugar regulation. Are you taking drugs for high blood pressure? Before starting a keto diet again, talk to the doctor. If you're breastfeeding, you shouldn't follow a ketogenic diet. Be mindful that limiting carbs will render you irritable, hungry, and sleepy, among other things. However, this may be a one-time occurrence. Keep in mind that you can eat a balanced diet in order to obtain all of the vitamins and minerals you need. A sufficient amount of fiber is also needed. When the body begins to derive energy from accumulated fat rather than glucose, it is said to be in ketosis. Several trials have shown the powerful weight-loss benefits of a low-carb, or keto, diet. This diet, on the other hand, can be difficult to stick to and can exacerbate health issues in individuals who have certain disorders, such as diabetes type 1. The keto diet is suitable for the majority of citizens. Nonetheless, all major dietary modifications should be discussed with a dietitian or doctor. This is essentially the case with people who have inherent conditions. The keto diet may be an effective therapy for people with drug-resistant epilepsy. Though the diet may be beneficial to people of any age, teenagers, people over 50, and babies can profit the most because they can easily stick to it. Modified keto diets, such as the revised Atkins diet or the low-glycemic index diet, are safer for adolescents and adults. A health care worker should keep a careful eye on someone who is taking a keto diet as a treatment. A doctor and dietitian will maintain track of a person's progress, administer drugs, and test for side effects. The body absorbs fat and protein differently than it does carbohydrates. Carbohydrates have a high insulin reaction. The protein sensitivity to insulin is mild, and the quick insulin response is negligible. Insulin is a fat-producing and fat-conserving enzyme. If you wish to lose weight, consume as many eggs, chickens, fish, and birds as you want, satiate yourself with the fat, and then eat every vegetable that grows on the ground.

Butter and coconut oil can be used instead of processed synthetic seed oils. You may be either a sugar or a fat burner, but not both.